W9-DGS-941

AMERICAN SAYINGS

AMERICAN SAYINGS

FAMOUS PHRASES · SLOGANS · AND
APHORISMS · BY HENRY F. WOODS

ESSENTIAL BOOKS

Duell, Sloan and Pearce   New York

FOR

LAURA CATHERINE

ACKNOWLEDGMENTS

In the preparation of this book I am indebted, for assistance of various kinds, to the following:

Lieutenant (jg) Roger W. Straus, Jr., Office of Public Relations, United States Navy; Miss Nora E. Cordingley, Harvard College Library; Mr. Christopher Morley; Miss Louella D. Everett; Mr. Stephen Early; Mr. James E. Craig, Chief Editorial Writer, New York *Sun;* Mr. John J. Noll, Associate Editor, *The American Legion Magazine;* Mr. George Morris, New York *News;* Mr. Floyd E. McCaffree, Republican National Committee; Miss Anna Hessel, *Richmond* (Virginia) *Times-Dispatch;* Miss Mary E. Woods; Mr. Julian P. Boyd, Princeton University Library; Reverend John J. Considine, M.M., Editor, *Far Afield;* Miss Lauretta Ravenna, New York *World-Telegram;* Henry F. Woods, Jr.; Fred E. Baer; Miss Lois M. Fawcett, Head of Reference Department, Minnesota Historical Society; First Lieutenant Ilma R. Ruohomaki, WAC, Chief, Army Information Service; Robert A. Hug, Newspaper Microfilm Dept., New York Public Library.

FOREWORD

IF THE songs of a people are potent to influence their ways, it is certain also that its slogans, watchwords, shibboleths, indicate the course of its history. American phrases which have had their origins in various fields of the Nation's activities—political, civil, social, economic—may be said to be footnotes to phases of its history. They have a significance, not so much in interpreting events to which they relate, as serving to remind us of the happenings that occasioned them.

Beginning with the first stirrings of popular discontent in the Colonies that culminated in the Revolution, it is evident that through our history the sententious phrase has been a favorite, reflecting, and sometimes influencing our moods and feelings. The power of a striking utterance, whether for good or evil, is indisputable. "Remember the Maine" probably was as effective in spurring this Nation to war against Spain as were old Cato's repeated thunderings against Carthage in inflaming the Roman people against the rival state in Africa.

The arrangement of this book is topical and chronological in each of the several classifications. Its purpose is to explain the origin and occasion of phrases and sayings which are or have been current in this country, which are frequently alluded to, or which are familiar to most Americans although they may have forgotten, or may never have known the identity of the authors or the occasions of the quotations. Some of the phrases quoted here differ slightly from the actual wording as originally uttered or written, but they are given in the altered forms because it is thus that they are popularly accepted, and because in most cases they are more pungently expressed, without changing the meaning of the original.

H. F. W.

New York.

CONTENTS

CONTENTS

PART ONE

POLITICAL AND CIVIL

"If the people be governors who shall be governed?"
John Cotton (*1585-1652*)

NEW ENGLAND'S people, who were among the first of the Colonists to wage a fight for the right to rule themselves, early in their history had to contend against a contrary theory of government held by some among their own numbers. The theocratic form of government of the Pilgrims who landed on Plymouth Rock was one of their own choosing, but they were nevertheless opposed to government by the few, aristocracy, and as Puritan government became more rigorous opposition increased.

John Cotton, a non-conformist minister who had fled England to escape the discipline of the established church for his views, was one of those in New England who had no faith in the common man. He advocated a strong government administered by a few, and in support of his theories he wrote and preached from his pulpit in Boston whither he had come in 1633.

"Democracy I do not conceive God ever did ordain as a fit government for either church or commonwealth," he wrote. "For if the people be governors who shall be governed? As for monarchy and aristocracy, they are both clearly approved and directed in the Scriptures."

Like Governor John Winthrop, Cotton, although self-exiled for the sake of freedom of conscience, maintained that the civil magistrates had power over the consciences of the governed, even to the extent of making them arbiters of life and death. Against these views Roger Williams spoke and wrote, and the controversy between him and Cotton led eventually to Williams' banishment and the founding of the Providence Plantations which, merged with other nearby settlements, became the Rhode Island colony.

"No taxation without representation."

(1765)

No PART of the fiscal program proposed by George Grenville, Prime Minister of Great Britain, to the parliamentary session of 1763-1764, was acceptable to the American colonists. The program was devised to raise revenue by duties on goods imported by the Colonies, and by the imposition of new taxes to be paid by the colonists. It was the contention of the ministries of George III that the people of his American possessions should be required to share in the expenses incurred in the defense, protection, and administration of the colonies by the mother country.

The colonists, however, denied the right of Parliament to tax them inasmuch as they were not represented in that body. James Otis declared that "Taxation without representation is tyranny," and "No taxation without representation" became a rallying cry in the agitation against the Stamp Act of 1765, the most objectionable of the measures enacted. This act, which was repealed in 1766, required that government stamps be affixed on newspapers and all legal documents executed in the colonies.

The tax program was inaugurated in 1764 with the enactment of the Sugar Act taxing certain imports, and this was followed by the Stamp Act. In 1767 Parliament passed the Customs Collecting Act, which established British Commissioners in the Colonies for the collection of customs and duties. In the same year a Revenue Act was passed, imposing taxes on lead, paint, and other items, and also the Tea Act, which gave a monopoly of exports of this article to the Colonies to the British East India Company.

"If this be treason, make the most of it."

Patrick Henry (1736-1739)

MORE THAN a decade before the signing of the Declaration of Independence an unmistakable note of revolution was sounded by Patrick Henry in the Virginia House of Burgesses.

In his speech on May 29, 1765, opposing the Stamp Act and avowing the right of the American colonies to assess their own taxes, the fiery orator said:

"Tarquin and Caesar each had his Brutus, Charles the First, his Cromwell, and George the Third—"

At this point he was interrupted by the Speaker's cry of "Treason".

And Henry resumed, "may profit by their example. If *this* be treason make the most of it."

*   *   *

"Give me liberty or give me death!"

Patrick Henry

CONCORD, LEXINGTON, AND BUNKER HILL were but a few weeks in the future when Patrick Henry's fervid oratory once again provided inspiration for American patriots. This time it was his speech before the Virginia Convention held in St. John's Episcopal Church, Richmond, on March 23, 1775. The closing sentences of that speech were:

"Is life so dear, or peace so sweet, as to be purchased at the price of chains and slavery? Forbid it, Almighty God! I know not what course others may take, but as for me, give me liberty or give me death!"

"We must indeed all hang together, or most assuredly
we will all hang separately."

Benjamin Franklin (1706-1790)

NONE OF the signers of the Declaration of Independence
underestimated the possible consequences to himself of
his act, and perhaps least of all did Benjamin Franklin.
He had been one of the committee appointed by the Congress to draft the resolution denouncing the oppressions
of the mother country and, with John Adams, had been
most active in working on it with Thomas Jefferson, to
whom had been assigned its actual composition. Franklin
had made several minor changes in the draft as completed by Jefferson, but they were merely in its phrase-
ology and did not in the least alter its momentous pur-
port. He realized as well as anyone that the document inevitably meant armed conflict.

The gravity of the step taken by the Congress, however, did not serve to suppress the quiet humor characteristic of him, and it was he who provided the one bit of
comic relief for the somber occasion of the signing of the
Declaration. As John Hancock signed he remarked: "We
must all be unanimous; there must be no pulling different ways; we must all hang together."

"Yes", Franklin replied. "We must indeed all hang together, or most assuredly we will all hang separately."

History is silent as to the other signers' reaction to the
grim pun, for the utterance of which we have the authority of only one of Franklin's biographers, Jared Sparks.
In his edition of Franklin's works he quotes the signer's
words "as also another anecdote related of Franklin."

"Proclaim liberty throughout all the land unto all the inhabitants thereof."

Old Testament

TOGETHER WITH the original drafts of the Declaration of Independence and the Constitution, the Liberty Bell is one of the most revered physical objects associated with the birth of the American Republic. The first bell to peal its notes of jubilation in Philadelphia over the adoption of the Declaration, it has ever since been cherished as the symbol of the freedom it proclaimed.

By a coincidence that now seems prophetic, the inscription it bears was ordered to be placed on it a quarter of a century before the Colonies had decided to cast themselves loose from the rule of the mother country. The bell, which was cast in England, was ordered by the Pennsylvania Provincial Assembly in 1751 for the new State House, and a committee of that body selected as the inscription for it words from Leviticus XXV, 10: "Proclaim liberty throughout all the land unto all the inhabitants thereof."

The bell was delivered in Philadelphia in 1752, but cracked while being tested for tone. It was recast in Philadelphia and hung in the State House on June 7, 1753. It remained there until September 1777, when it was removed to Allentown, Pennsylvania, where it was secreted to prevent its falling into the hands of the British. In June 1778, it was returned to Philadelphia, and thereafter it was rung on the anniversary of the Declaration of Independence. In 1835, it was cracked while tolling as the body of Chief Justice Marshall was being taken to Virginia. It is now enshrined in the hallway of the old State House in Philadelphia.

"He snatched the lightning from heaven and the sceptre from tyrants."

Anne Robert Jacques Turgot (1727-1781)

PROBABLY no American has ever received the acclaim given Banjamin Franklin by the French people. Almost certainly none retained their undiminished admiration to the last as he did. Not only was his company and conversation sought after and esteemed by statesmen, economists, scientists, philosophers, and men and women of letters, but he was the pet of the ladies of the court, and his many portraits made his features probably as familiar to the people of Paris as those of their sovereign. He was overwhelmed by requests from painters and sculptors to sit to them for portraits and busts, but was obliged to refuse most of them.

One of the French artists for whom he consented to sit in 1778 was Jean-Antoine Houdon, whose fine bust of George Washington, executed after that of Franklin, is in the capitol of Richmond, Virginia. Among Franklin's closest friends in Paris was the statesman and economist, Anne Robert Jacques Turgot, controller-general of France. He wrote the famous inscription for the Houdon bust of Franklin: *"Eripuit coelo fulmen sceptrumque tyrannis"* ("He snatched the lightning from heaven and the sceptre from tyrants.") In his epigram Turgot expressed his admiration for his friend's scientific experiments which identified the electrical nature of lightning, and for his part, as one of the signers of the Declaration of Independence, in freeing the Colonies from oppressive British rule.

Franklin himself, always conservative in speech, modestly believed, that Turgot's Gallic enthusiasm did him too much credit, especially as to his overthrowing tyrants, for he said he was only one of many who had accomplished the Revolution.

"Where liberty dwells, there is my country."

Benjamin Franklin

TWENTY-FIVE of Benjamin Franklin's eighty-four years of life were spent abroad in the service of his country. For five years, from 1757 to 1762, he resided in England as the agent there of Pennsylvania, and in 1864 he returned to England in the same capacity and vigorously opposed the Stamp Act. After eleven years in England he returned to America in 1775, when armed revolt was flaring up in the Colonies.

After assisting in the drafting of the Declaration of Independence, he was sent as one of the Commissioners, with Arthur Lee and Silas Deane, to France to enlist the support of that country for the Revolution. There he remained for nine years, accomplishing deeds of incalculable value to the struggling Colonies. His return to America in 1785 was in compliance with his wish to retire from public life, and it was at this time that in a letter he expressed the thought of a man long absent from his native land: "Where liberty dwells, there is my country."

But the call of his country upon his services could not be denied, and in 1789 he was chosen as a delegate to the Convention that drew up the Constitution of the Federal Union. Even after the Constitution had been ratified, he continued to work in the cause of freedom. He became president of the Abolition Society, and in the year of his death his last public act was the signing of a petition to the Congress praying the immediate abolition of slavery in the United States and the suppression of the slave-trade.

"A more perfect union."

The Constitution of the United States

THE ARTICLES OF CONFEDERATION under which the Continental Congress functioned up to the adoption of the Constitution were deemed generally a loose and unsatisfactory union of the States which formed the new nation. Until "a more perfect union" should be accomplished it was recognized by the builders of the Republic that a truly stable government could not be hoped for.

The main underlying purpose of the Constitution is expressed in the first fifteen words of its opening sentence: "We the People of the United States, in Order to form a more perfect union . . ."

*   *   *

"First in war, first in peace, first in the hearts of his countrymen."

Henry Lee (1756-1818)

PERHAPS THE most memorable funeral oration ever delivered in this country was that by Henry Lee of Virginia before the Congress after the death of Washington, December 14, 1799. Lee had served under Washington in the War of the Revolution, and as a dashing and successful scout and outpost leader became famous as "Light Horse Harry." He was deeply attached to the first President, and his eulogy of him, in which he used the phrase, "first in war, first in peace, first in the hearts of his countrymen", was characterized by sincerity and depth of feeling. Lee was the father of Robert E. Lee, the Confederate general.

"George Washington—the Joshua, who commanded the sun and the moon to stand still, and they obeyed him."
Benjamin Franklin

BENJAMIN FRANKLIN'S vein of dry humor was so pronounced that, according to one of his biographers, it was only because his colleagues in the Continental Congress feared that he might introduce a joke into the Declaration of Independence that he was not selected to draft that document. Instead, the task was assigned to Thomas Jefferson, who was assisted by a drafting committee of which Franklin was an active member.

The venerable statesman-philosopher-scientist was held in affectionate esteem by his fellow members in the Congress and in the Constitutional Convention. The relations between Washington and Franklin were especially cordial, and each had for the other a great admiration. Illustrative of the high regard Franklin entertained for the Republic's first President is the anecdote related of Franklin by his biographer, James Parton. While Parton does not vouch for its authenticity, the incident might very well have happened and the anecdote has the character of Frankin's wit.

As related by Parton, Franklin was present at an official dinner at which the ambassadors of Great Britain and France were also guests. When toasts were called for the British ambassador proposed: "England—the sun—whose bright beams enlighten and fructify the remotest corners of the earth."

In turn the ambassador of France proposed his toast: "France—the moon—whose mild, steady, and cheering rays are the delight of all nations, consoling them in darkness."

When Franklin was called upon, he pledged his toast in these words: "George Washington—the Joshua, who commanded the sun and the moon to stand still, and they obeyed him."

"Millions for Defense, But Not One Cent for Tribute."

Robert Goodloe Harper (1765-1825)

THE MOOT question of the French-American Treaty of 1778 continued to disturb the relations of the two countries when the terms of the Jay treaty with Great Britain in 1794 became generally known. While the treaty averted war with England, it was not received with unqualified favor in this country, and certainly not in France. England had agreed to the American demands on several points affecting territorial disputes and indemnities for damages to American shipping, but refused to make any concessions regarding our trade with the West Indies whose ports France had opened to neutral trade. England, then at war with France, ordered the seizure of neutral vessels carrying food supplies to France or her colonies.

The French Directory viewed Jay's treaty as a violation of our Treaty of 1778 with France, and resented our refusal to join her in her war with England. The French government in December 1796, refused to receive the newly appointed American minister, Charles C. Pinckney, and began to attack American shipping. President John Adams, desirous of avoiding war with France, sent John Marshall and Elbridge Gerry to France to help Pinckney reach an agreement with the French government.

The American commissioners were told by a French official that if they wanted Pinckney to be received as minister they would have to bribe certain designated officials in the French government, the sum of $250,000 being named as the total of the bribe money. Pinckney's answer was an unequivocal refusal to bribe any official of the government, and the commissioners were ordered by President Adams to return home. Congress then declared the Treaty of 1778 abrogated, the nation was aroused when the details of the "X Y Z Affair" became known, the letters indicating the unnamed French officials who had solicited the bribe, and a warlike feeling gained throughout the country.

The legend that Pinckney's refusal was phrased in the haughty words, "Millions for defense, but not one cent for tribute," was denied by Pinckney himself, who is quoted as saying "No, my answer was not a flourish like that, but simply, 'Not a penny! Not a penny!'" The popular version was credited to Robert Goodloe Harper of South Carolina by the *American Daily Advertiser,* which in its issue of June 20, 1798, published it as one of sixteen toasts proposed at a dinner given by the Congress to John Marshall in June 1798 upon his return from France.

From midsummer of 1798 until the end of 1799 this country and France were in state of actual, if undeclared war, and French cruisers captured more than eighty American ships during that period.

The French Directory was overthrown by Napoleon's coup of November 10, 1799, and as First Consul the Corsican became master of France. On a hint from Talleyrand, French foreign minister, President Adams reopened negotiations with the French government, and by a convention signed September 30, 1800, France agreed to the abrogation of the Treaty of 1778 in return for the abandonment by this country of all claims on France for damages done to American shipping by French cruisers since 1793.

"Stand with Washington."

(1796)

GEORGE WASHINGTON's election and re-election were by unanimous vote. Fittingly, he was not the candidate of any party, but the undisputed choice of a grateful nation. But though there were no political parties at this stage of the young Republic's history, there were differing theories and concepts of government that inevitably would crystalize into political organizations. Indeed, in Washington's first term there were two opposing factions in the process of forming, both represented in the President's cabinet: Alexander Hamilton, Secretary of the Treasury, for the Federalists, and Thomas Jefferson, Secretary of State, for the Republicans.

By the time of Washington's second administration these parties were fairly launched. Of the two, the Federalist was the stronger and better organized. That party composed of the followers of Jefferson, believers in a purely democratic government as opposed to a monarchical or aristocratic form, was as yet loosely knit, without even the name Republican by which it came to be known.

As long as Hamilton and Jefferson remained in the cabinet, which was for the greater part of Washington's first term, they were at odds on almost every point in government policy. Hamilton's views on the implied powers of the Constitution, a strong centralized government, and his unconcealed distrust of the masses were contrary to Jefferson's belief in State sovereignty, a government after the French republican model, and his abiding confidence in the people and their right to rule. Both men continued the acknowledged leaders of their respective parties after their retirement from the cabinet, and the political cleavage in the Nation widened.

Although Washington was of no party, he leaned to the political ideas of the Federalists, and the cry "Stand with Washington" was repeatedly raised whenever the

Federalists sought popular support for measures they advocated. Until the passing of the Federalist party with the defeat of John Adams by Jefferson, this appeal was often effective, such was the magic of Washington's name.

*   *   *

"Our country, right or wrong."
Stephen Decatur (1779-1820)

COMMODORE DECATUR, already a naval hero, became a popular idol upon his return in 1816 from a punitive expedition to the Barbary Coast of North Africa. He had sailed from New York in May, 1815, in command of a squadron of nine ships to demand redress from the pirate rulers of the North African coast for depredations upon American commerce. He had forced the Dey of Algiers to sign a treaty ending the payment of tribute to him by the American government and promising full payment for injuries inflicted upon Americans by Algerian pirates. Next he had forced the rulers of Tunis and Tripoli to indemnify Americans for injuries suffered at their hands since 1812.

Decatur was feted in cities throughout the United States. At one of these dinners in Norfolk, Virginia, he proposed the toast:

"Our Country! In her intercourse with foreign governments may she always be in the right; but our country, right or wrong."

Carl Schurz in an address in 1872 in Congress, thus paraphrased Decatur's toast: "Our country, right or wrong. When right to be kept right, when wrong to be put right."

"Entangling alliances with none."

> *Thomas Jefferson (1743-1826)*

CONTRARY TO a widely prevalent belief, this phrase originated with Jefferson, not with George Washington. As Secretary of State in the cabinet of the first President, Jefferson denied the plea of the French government for permission to use American territory as a base for the purchase of munitions and the fitting out of expeditions against the forces of England, Prussia, Austria, and Spain, with which nations the French were, in 1793, at war.

France had called upon the American government to live up to the Treaty of 1778, which was one of alliance. Washington recognized the republican government of France, but announced that the United States would be neutral. The phrase, penned in full by Jefferson, whose sympathy with the French Revolution was ardent and outspoken, is: "Peace, commerce, and honest friendship for all nations, entangling alliances with none," and occurs in his first inaugural address.

* * *

"We must marry ourselves to the British fleet and nation."

> *Thomas Jefferson*

NEWS OF the cession in 1800 by Spain to France of the entire basin of the Mississippi, called Louisiana, did not reach President Jefferson until the Spring of 1802. It was disturbing news, for Jefferson could not view without uneasiness the prospect of the transfer from a feeble nation like Spain to powerful France the west bank of the Mississippi River, through which passed the commerce of nearly one quarter of the United States.

Although no lover of England, the President expressed his concern to Robert Livingston, American minister in Paris, to whom he wrote that "the moment Napoleon takes possession of New Orleans we must marry ourselves to the British fleet and nation."

"The Era of Good Feeling."

(1817)

JAMES MONROE became President in 1817 at an auspicious period in American history. The experience of the War of 1812 had served to turn the minds of Americans from any dependence on Europe and to convince them that in a nationalist policy lay the country's real future.

The war ended in 1814 and by 1815 peace prevailed generally throughout the world. For the better part of Monroe's two terms as President he was more fortunate than most Presidents before or since in accomplishing results with a minimum of opposition. "The Era of Good Feeling," as the period became known, was marked by the acquisition of Florida from Spain, the admission of five new states into the Union, the passage of the Missouri Compromise which it was fondly hoped by many had settled the controversy over slavery, and last, but by no means least, the enunciation of the Monroe Doctrine which had the support of all elements in the country, irrespective of party affiliations.

* * *

"To the victors belong the spoils."

William Learned Marcy (1786-1857)

THIS INDORSEMENT of the policy of rewarding faithful party members with public offices was uttered by Senator Marcy, of New York, in a speech delivered in the United States Senate in January 1832. Marcy, replying to a speech by Henry Clay attacking President Van Buren for his bestowal of favors upon his supporters, declared that the Democrats "see nothing wrong in the rule that to the victors belong the spoils of the enemy."

His defense of the spoils system caused widespread criticism of him, but did not affect his political fortunes adversely, for subsequently he served three terms as governor of New York, and in 1843, became Secretary of War.

"A corrupt bargain."

Andrew Jackson (1767-1845)

IN THE presidential campaign of 1824 none of the four candidates—John Quincy Adams, Andrew Jackson, William H. Crawford and Henry Clay—received a majority of the electoral votes and the election consequently was thrown into the House. Clay, having received the smallest number of votes, was eliminated by the Constitution from the voting for President.

Although Clay had carried his own state, Kentucky, overwhelmingly against Andrew Jackson, his nearest competitor, the Kentucky legislature instructed him to cast his vote in the House for Jackson. Clay, however, voted for John Quincy Adams, who was elected. This enraged Jackson and his followers, who charged that Clay's action was in fulfillment of a "corrupt bargain", and when Adams made Clay his Secretary of State the Jacksonians cited this as proof of the truth of their charges.

It was probably in allusion to this allegation that John Randolph of Virginia in a speech excoriating Clay said of him: "So brilliant, yet so corrupt, like a rotten mackerel by moonlight, shines and stinks."

"Independence now and forever!"

John Adams (1735-1826)

As JOHN ADAMS lay dying on the morning of July 4, 1826, the fiftieth anniversary of the signing of the Declaration of Independence, he was aroused by the firing of cannon in the street near by. When told that it was in celebration of Independence Day, he murmured, "Independence forever!"

Four days before he had been asked for a toast to be given in his name at a Fourth of July celebration. He replied with the following: "It is my living sentiment, and by the blessing of God it shall be my dying sentiment,— Independence now and Independence forever!"

In Daniel Webster's eulogy of Adams and Jefferson, delivered in Boston on August 2, 1826, he supposed the speech that Adams might have made in supporting his vote for the adoption by the Continental Congress of the Declaration of Independence, and used this toast as the peroration of the supposed speech.

"Sink or swim, live or die, survive or perish, I give my hand and my heart to this vote."

Daniel Webster (1782-1852)

JOHN ADAMS died on July 4, 1826, and Thomas Jefferson's death ensued a few hours later on the same day. Sorrow at the passing of these two eminent patriots and former Presidents was widespread, and the City Council of Boston ordered a memorial service to be held in Faneuil Hall, on August 2, at which Daniel Webster was invited to deliver the commemorative address.

In a moving eulogy Webster sketched the careers of Adams and Jefferson and their services in the creation of the Republic, with emphasis on the part they had taken in framing the Declaration of Independence. He drew a word picture of the scene in the Continental Congress on the day of the final debate, held in a closed session, on the adoption of the Declaration.

To the words of caution he imagined John Hancock to have spoken, Webster opposed those which Adams might have uttered in supporting a severance by the Colonies of the ties with the mother country. Adams' supposed speech, as imagined by Webster, which accorded with his known sentiments, gave a ringing assent to the adoption of the Declaration of Independence in the words: "Sink or swim, live or die, survive or perish, I give my hand and my heart to this vote."

"Thomas Jefferson still lives."

John Adams

IN THEIR years of retirement Thomas Jefferson and John Adams, who had been rivals in public life, were reconciled and on terms of almost affectionate esteem, regularly exchanging letters. They had been equally zealous in their work for the cause of independence and had been associated on the committee of the Continental Congress that drew up the Declaration of Independence. Both had assisted in the formation of a nation and had been officially identified with the government of the young republic, Adams as Vice President under Washington, then as President; Jefferson, as Secretary of State during part of Washington's first administration, and successively Vice President and President.

But in their political beliefs they were far apart, for the Federalist concept of government to which Adams held was opposed at nearly every point to the democratic doctrine in which Jefferson believed. This could not fail to affect, in some measure, their personal relations, which were further strained by the Alien and Sedition acts in Adams' administration, in which Jefferson was Vice President.

Yet neither of the rivals overlooked the purity of character, the patriotism, and the civic virtues of the other. The mellowing of age and their withdrawal from the turmoil of politics served to do away with partisan asperities and to revive their respect and esteem for each other. While neither abjured any part of his political principles, each conceded the integrity of the other's beliefs and their correspondence was conducted on the high plane of philosophical discussion.

Just before he died Adams murmured, "Thomas Jefferson still lives."

Jefferson had died earlier that day, but his friend's dying words were prophetic of the endurance of Jefferson's name and his political doctrines.

"Liberty and Union, now and forever, one and inseparable!"

Daniel Webster

THE CONTENTION that a state in the American Union had the right under the Constitution to suspend within the state a federal law was not formally enunciated until resolutions adopted by Virginia and Kentucky, in 1798 and 1799, set forth this interpretation. The Kentucky resolution further declared the right of a state to nullify federal laws. Pennsylvania, in 1809, actually supported its voiding of a federal decree by calling out the state militia to prevent the execution of the laws that were objected to. The unpopular Embargo law of the national government was declared invalid in New England in 1809-1810; and Georgia in 1825-1829, and Alabama in 1832-1835, nullified federal laws relating to the Indians.

The action of the South Carolina legislature, declaring the high tariff act of 1828, the "tariff of abominations," unconstitutional, led to the great Hayne-Webster debate in the Senate early in 1830, when Robert Y. Hayne of South Carolina upheld the right of his State to declare void a federal law. Daniel Webster of Massachusetts in his speech of January 26 and 27, replying to Hayne, reached a climax in his fame as orator and authority upon the Constitution.

Upholding the nationalist concept of the Union, Webster eloquently praised it, declaring that its existence antedated that of the states; that the people had framed the Constitution, not as a compact, but as an instrument for the creation of a power sovereign within the limits of assigned powers, and that the Supreme Court was the sole arbiter of the extent of these powers. He denied the right of a State to declare a federal law void and, asserting that nullification could result only in violence and civil war, he declared that he was for "Liberty *and* Union, now and forever, one and inseparable!"

"Our Federal Union! It must and shall be preserved."
Andrew Jackson

THIS WAS Andrew Jackson's challenge to John C. Calhoun, Vice President in Jackson's first administration, delivered as a toast at a Jefferson birthday dinner on April 30, 1830. The echoes of the Webster-Hayne debate in the Senate on the issue of nullification and State rights, as set forth in the "South Carolina Exposition," had not yet died away.

At the dinner President Jackson was called upon for a toast. Lifting his glass, the President looked straight at Calhoun, author of the South Carolina document, and proposed the toast which unequivocally declared Jackson's attitude on the question of nullification.

The Vice President's reply was phrased in the toast: "The Union—next to our liberty most dear—may we all remember that it can be preserved only by respecting the rights of the states."

Jackson's long feud with Calhoun was not forgotten even in Old Hickory's retirement from public life. Several years before his death he is reported to have expressed two regrets: that he could not have had Henry Clay shot and John Calhoun hung. While nullification sentiment was raging in South Carolina, President Jackson prior to the issuance of his Proclamation on Nullification warned nullifiers that if a single drop of blood were shed in that state over this issue he would hang every nullifier that he "could get [his] hands on."

"I will not retreat a single inch, and I will be heard."
William Lloyd Garrison (1805-1879)

IN WILLIAM LLOYD GARRISON, a young journeyman printer turned journalist, the radical wing of the Abolitionist movement found its most vigorous and powerful voice. Garrison advocated immediate emancipation of the slaves. His extreme views, as expressed in the columns of *The Genius of Universal Emancipation,* of which he was assistant editor, caused his conviction in 1830 in Baltimore, where the paper was published, on a charge of libel. Upon his release from jail after seven weeks, when his fine was paid by a symphathizer, he went on a lecture tour of Northern cities.

Although public sentiment against the institution of slavery was growing the extremists among Abolitionists made many foes for the movement, and their foremost spokesman was an object of hatred in the North as well as in the South. On New Year's Day of 1831, Garrison began publication in Boston of *The Liberator.* In the salutatory of the first number he wrote: "On this subject I do not wish to think, or speak, or write with moderation. . . . I will be harsh as truth and as uncompromising as justice. . . . I am in earnest—I will not equivocate—I will not excuse—I will not retreat a single inch—and I will be heard."

This bold statement aroused renewed hostility toward him. He was widely denounced as a "fanatic" and as "a public enemy." His life was threatened in hundreds of letters. A reward of $5,000 was offered by the State of Georgia for his arrest and prosecution, and in 1835 he was dragged through the streets of Boston, with a rope around his neck, by a mob which broke up one of his meetings. He was rescued by the police and lodged in jail for protection. But Garrison was heard. And the ringing words of his salutatory are inscribed on his monument in Boston.

"Two Dollars a Day and Roast Beef."

(1836)

THE ADMINISTRATION of President Van Buren was darkened by a financial panic which lasted throughout his term. The Whig party conducted its campaign for its nominees, Harrison and Tyler, on the issue of prosperity and made liberal use of slogans, songs, and other appeals which were the forerunners of today's campaign methods. A popular cry, ancestor of the "Full Dinner Pail" slogan in the McKinley campaign many years later, was: "Van's Policy, Fifty Cents a Day and French Soup: Our Policy, Two Dollars a Day and Roast Beef."

Elaborate descriptions of the luxurious mode of life and sybaritic tastes attributed to Van Buren by his political foes were broadcast. Contrasted with these were the simple ways of Harrison, symbolized by representations of a lowly log cabin and cider jug. In point of fact, Harrison was the possessor of inherited wealth and lived in a mansion.

* * *

"Tippecanoe and Tyler too."

(1836)

WILLIAM HENRY HARRISON was elected ninth President in 1836 on a gallant, though minor, military record. As governor of Indian Territory in 1800 he endeavored to avert hostilities with the Indians, but was compelled to take the field against Chief Tecumseh, and at the battle of Tippecanoe, November 7, 1811, he beat off a fierce attack of the Indians.

His running mate in the presidential campaign was John Tyler, included in the cry, "Tippecanoe and Tyler too." In this campaign mass meetings, processions, banners, emblems, and the various devices now a familiar accompaniment of political contests were used for the first time.

"John Marshall has made his decision, now let him en-
force it."

Andrew Jackson

LIKE MANY persons of forceful character, Andrew Jackson
could be inconsistent on occasion. Also, like Presidents before and after him, he did not always agree with the decisions handed down by the Supreme Court of the United
States and was not hesitant about expressing his dissent.

The notable instance of this was his declaration that,
"John Marshall has made his decision, now let him en-
force it," after the Chief Justice had read the decision of
the Supreme Court adverse to a cause supported by
Jackson.

The State of Georgia annexed the territories of the
Creek and Cherokee Indians within its borders after having vainly endeavored to induce the Indians to withdraw
from Georgia. The Indians' possession of the lands had
been guaranteed to them by Federal treaty, but Georgia
ignored the treaty. Jackson who had on a prior occasion
boldly denied this right of a state to nullify a Federal law,
sent a message to the Congress upholding the State.

The case came before the Supreme Court on a writ of
error. Two New England missionaries had been sentenced
to prison by a state court for their refusal to comply with
a state law requiring white persons in the Cherokee territories in Georgia to take an oath of allegiance to the state.
When the writ of error issued by the Supreme Court was
served on the Governor of Georgia that official denied the
Court's authority.

The missionaries' case was argued before the Court in
February 1832. The judgment of the Georgia court was
reversed. The Supreme Court held that the Federal gov-
ernment had exclusive jurisdiction over Indian lands. The
State refused to obey the mandate and was upheld by
Jackson, whose comment on Marshall was attributed to

him by Horace Greeley. The Indians were removed to lands west of the Mississippi.

Jackson's disagreement with Marshall apparently left no bitter memory with him, for when the Chief Justice died his erstwhile political foe said of him that he was one of "the greatest men of his age."

* * *

"A covenant with death and an agreement with hell."
William Lloyd Garrison

THIS WAS Garrison's characterization of the Constitution of the United States in answer to those moderates among the Abolitionists who held that the Constitution sanctioned slavery where it was already established. Garrison's intemperate statement was incorporated in resolutions drafted by him and adopted by the Massachusetts Anti-Slavery Society on January 27, 1843.

Garrison and extremist Abolitionists insisted that slavery was sin, a crime, and a violation of the Christian principle of the brotherhood of man. Consistent with his declaration that the Constitution itself was an evil instrument, he burned a copy of it at an open air celebration of Abolitionists in Framingham, Massachusetts, on July 4, 1854.

"I name thee Old Glory!"

William Driver (1803-1886)

MORE THAN a century ago the flag received the name by which it is affectionately known to Americans everywhere. The honor of bestowing the name Old Glory to it belongs to a young sea captain, William Driver, of Salem, Massachusetts. Prior to sailing out of Salem in 1831 on a voyage to the South Pacific as master of the brig *Charles Dogget,* a large American flag was presented to Driver, who had it run up on the masthead. As the bunting was broken out to the breeze, Driver saluted it with the words: "I name thee Old Glory!"

Driver treasured the flag and when he retired from the sea to reside in Nashville, Tennessee, the flag went with him. He was an ardent supporter of the Union and early in the Civil War he did not hestitate to fly the flag from a window of his house, a daring thing to do in a city where adherents of the Confederacy predominated. Several attempts were made by the more ardent among the latter to seize the flag, but repeated searches of the house and grounds failed to discover it, for Driver had concealed it by having it sewed within the coverlet of his bed.

When Nashville was captured by Union forces in 1862 Old Glory was brought out from its hiding place and flown from the dome of the state capitol in Nashville. On that occasion Driver again greeted the flag as "Old Glory." It is now in the Smithsonian Institution in Washington.

According to George Henry Preble, a naval officer who served in the war and later wrote *A History of the Flag of the United States,* the Stars and Stripes were commonly known to Union soldiers as Old Glory during the Civil War.

"One Country, One Constitution, and One Destiny."
Daniel Webster

THE DANGERS that threatened a break-up of the Federal Union had been foreseen early by Daniel Webster. In his great debate in the Senate with Robert Y. Hayne, of South Carolina, Webster had eloquently denied any interpretation of the Constitution which gave a state the right to nullify a federal law, and he consistently viewed the Constitution as an instrument for the perpetuation of the Union. In his speeches and in his public life he was a valiant and powerful pleader for the continued unity of the people and an enduring Republic, and he was regarded throughout the nation as a foremost champion of the Constitution.

He had received the electoral vote of Massachusetts for President in 1836, and although unsuccessful, he was still the idol of a large section of the Whig Party, members of which invited him to deliver an address at a public meeting in Niblo's Saloon, New York City, on March 15, 1837.

Webster on this occasion devoted a large part of his address to a laudation of the Constitution and an eloquent plea for the perpetuity of the Union, upon whose continuance, he declared, depended in great measure the liberties of Americans, as well as of those of peoples everywhere. He concluded a logical explanation of the necessity for the Union with the words:

"Let us then stand by the Constitution as it is, and by our Country as it is, one, united, and entire; let it be a truth engraven on the flag under which we rally in every contingency, that we have One Country, One Constitution, and One Destiny."

"Fifty-four Forty or Fight."

William Allen (1806-1879)

OREGON, UNDER which name originally was included all the territory between the Rocky Mountains and the Pacific Ocean north of 42 degrees north latitude, threatened in 1844 to be a cause of war between this country and Great Britain. The latter country claimed the territory, but in 1818 a treaty of joint occupation was agreed to between the two claimants, and it lasted until 1846.

By 1844, however, many Americans had settled in the territory, expansionist sentiment was growing throughout the nation, and extension of the Oregon boundary farther north as far as the southern boundary of Alaska became an issue in the presidential election of 1844. In the campaign to elect James K. Polk to the presidency the catch phrase "Fifty-four Forty or Fight" became a favorite slogan. The phrase was attributed to Senator William Allen, of Ohio, a forceful figure in the Senate who counted among his nicknames that of "Earthquake Allen."

In the end "fifty-four forty" was not the boundary accepted by us, and there was no fight, for both sides to the controversy were willing to compromise. In June 1846 by a treaty signed with Great Britain it was agreed to divide the region in dispute almost equally between the two claimants, fixing the boundary at the forty-ninth parallel, except the Island of Vancouver, which went to England.

The States of Washington, Oregon, and Idaho are embraced in what was once the territory of Oregon.

"I would rather be right than be President."

Henry Clay (1777-1852)

HENRY CLAY, of Kentucky, in his lifetime known as the "President Maker," five times unsuccessfully sought to be President. In 1824 he was a candidate, but saw the coveted office go to John Quincy Adams. In 1832 he was the nominee of the Whigs but he lost to Andrew Jackson by an overwhelming vote. Eight years later he sought to be again the Whigs' nominee, but had to yield to General William Henry Harrison. Once more, in 1844, he reached for the elusive office when he ran against James K. Polk, of Tennessee, who was elected. Clay's final effort, in 1848, was lost to General Zachary Taylor.

Bitterly disappointed though he was, Clay rose above personal ambitions and bent his efforts to avert the outbreak of civil war over slavery and State rights. He had been re-elected to the Senate in 1848 and he introduced a series of resolutions known as the Compromises of 1850, designed to reconcile sectional differences on questions affecting the institution of slavery.

In the course of a speech on the Compromises, replying to a taunt about his unsuccessful quest of the Presidency, he made the statement that he "would rather be right than be President."

"Our manifest destiny is to overspread the continent."

John Louis O'Sullivan (1813-1895)

EXPANSIONIST STIRRINGS in the United States, which began early in the nation's history, were quickened measurably by the break-up of Spain's empire in South America during the luckless reign of Ferdinand VII. In that period Spain lost every one of its colonies in continental America, and of all its possessions in the Western Hemisphere only Cuba and Porto Rico remained to her.

Cuba, "The Pearl of the Antilles," was coveted by American expansionists for varying reasons. Those in the South desired its acquisition for the extension of slavery territory. Because of its strategic importance and as the largest island in the Caribbean, others believed it vital to the national safety that it be acquired by this country. The concern of our government was mainly that Cuba should remain a Spanish possession safe from the designs of other foreign powers. But as the belief grew among Americans that an island so close to us was destined to be acquired by us, an offer of $10,000,000 for Cuba was made to Spain, which refused to sell it.

Extension of the territorial limits of the United States to the Southwest, to the Pacific, and California was regarded by most Americans as inevitable, but the first known use of the term "manifest destiny" is found in the *United States Magazine and Democratic Review* of July-August 1845. In condemnation of the opposition to the annexation of Texas, John Louis O'Sullivan, editor of the magazine, declared:

"Our manifest destiny is to overspread the continent allotted by Providence for the free development of our yearly multiplying millions."

Thereafter the use of the term in the sense that O'Sullivan had employed it was favored by American expansionists whether known as such or by the latter designation of imperialists. When this country annexed Hawaii,

President McKinley in a private conversation remarked of it that it was "manifest destiny."

* * *

"This is the last of earth! I am content."

John Quincy Adams (1767-1848)

IT WAS as John Quincy Adams could have wished, that he should die in harness after a long life filled with public services of great value to his country. The sixth President of the United States after holding the high office that his father, John Adams, had held, against all precedent he became a Representative in the Congress from his native State Massachusetts. There he served for seventeen years, so powerful a voice in advocacy of causes and measures he favored that he was known as "The Old Man Eloquent."

While in his seat on the floor of the House he was stricken with paralysis on February 21, 1848. Four days later he died, on his lips the words: "This is the last of earth! I am content."

Probably no man of his time had better reason than Adams to be satisfied with his life work. In the House he had won his nine-years' fight for the abolition of the so-called "Gag Rules" of that body which were directed against the right of petition opposed by the advocates of slavery. Before his election to the Presidency in 1824 he had been minister, successively, to The Hague, Portugal, and Prussia; a member of the Massachusetts State Senate and of the United States Senate; minister to Russia, then to England. In 1817, he became Secretary of State in the administration of President Monroe, and it was through his office that the Monroe Doctrine was enunciated. The actual authorship of this famous document was credited by many to John Quincy Adams.

"I know no South, no North, no East, no West, to which I owe any allegiance."

Henry Clay

OMINOUS SIGNS threatening the dissolution of the Union were showing long before the secession of 1860. The vexed question of slavery, the conflicting interpretations of the Constitution, agitation of the doctrine of State rights and, in general, the increase of sectional jealousies and prejudices were disturbing to those who had at heart the perpetuation of the Union.

Henry Clay, although a Kentuckian, Virginia-born, was among the staunchest advocates of the Federal Union, and opposed to the extreme sectionalism exemplified by John C. Calhoun of South Carolina. But Clay's policy was one of compromise, a position in regard to slavery that had cost him the presidency in 1842.

In 1850, seeking to avert national disruption, he introduced in the Senate the Compromise of 1850, designed to allay the growing friction between the North and South. It was in the debate on these that, taking note of sectional jealousies, he said: "Sir, I have heard something said on this and a former occasion about allegiance to the South. I know no South, no North, no East, no West to which I owe any allegiance. I owe allegiance to two sovereignties, and only two: one is to the sovereignty of this Union, and the other is the sovereignty of the state of Kentucky."

The Compromise of 1850 was a real contribution to the solidarity of the Union, even though it did not have the effect of averting the "irrepressible conflict."

"Eternal vigilance is the price of liberty."

Wendell Phillips (1811-1884)

FREEDOM OF speech, as well as that of human beings from physical bondage, was a cherished ideal of Wendell Phillips, ardent abolitionist and eloquent pleader. While a young lawyer practicing in his native Boston, he became in 1835, at the mobbing in Boston of William Lloyd Garrison, leader of the anti-slavery movement in New England. Garrison had refused to be silenced by the threats of violence, and his meeting was broken up and he was hauled through the streets to jail.

From that time Phillips devoted himself wholeheartedly to the cause of the abolition of slavery, speaking on many occasions, at the eventual cost of the loss of his legal practice. His earnestness and moving oratory made him valuable to the cause and he was much in demand for public addresses in its support. The striking phrase, "Eternal vigilance is the price of liberty," was used in his address, *Public Opinion,* delivered before the Massachusetts Anti-Slavery Society on January 28, 1852. It had been attributed to Thomas Jefferson, but Phillips in a letter written in 1879, asserted that no one had yet found it in Jefferson's works "or elsewhere." Patrick Henry also had been credited with the quotation, with similar lack of proof.

"Free soil, free men, free speech, Fré-mont."

(1856)

John C. Frémont, "The Pathfinder," was the first nominee for President of the newly formed Republican party which grew out of the protracted slavery controversy. The first national nominating committee, meeting in Philadelphia on June 17, 1856, named him to run against James Buchanan, the candidate of the Democrats.

Frémont was a picturesque figure who had gained prominence because of notable expeditions in Oregon and California in the period between 1842 and 1848, and was a rabid opponent of slavery. The nominating committee adopted a platform which called upon the Congress to legislate for the abolition of the "twin relics of barbarism," slavery and polygamy.

The slogan used in the campaign was indicative of the principal issues in it, but it was not potent to cause Frémont's election.

* * *

"Let us have peace."

Ulysses Simpson Grant (1822-1885)

As ONE who knew the horrors of war in general and in particular of that in which he had fought to final victory, Grant was undoubtedly sincere in the desire for peace which he expressed in his speech of acceptance of the Republican nomination for President on May 29, 1868.

His party, in adopting the policy of reconstruction that treated the South as a conquered province and in its unsuccessful attempt to impeach President Johnson because of his lack of sympathy for its program, was hardly promoting peace. Yet its candidate ventured to declare for it.

"An irrepressible conflict."

William Henry Seward (1801-1872)

TWO YEARS before the outbreak of the Civil War, William Henry Seward, who was destined to have an important part in it, foresaw it as inevitable. Twice governor of New York and United States Senator for two terms from that state, Seward had been a consistent opponent of slavery and had frequently voiced his opinion about the system. He had opposed the admission of Texas into the Union, declaring that "To maintain a slave-holding power is to subvert the Union." Also in the campaign of 1848 he had said of slavery, "It must be abolished."

Probably no pronouncement of his on slavery, however, created the sensation throughout the nation caused by his speech at Rochester, New York, on October 25, 1858. In the course of that address, speaking of the situation presented by the Dred Scott decision of the Supreme Court that held slaves to be property, Seward spoke of "an irrepressible conflict between opposing and enduring forces."

The striking phrase caused widespread comment, and some criticism on the part of those who believed that the slavery problem could be solved without recourse to arms.

"It is not best to swap horses while crossing the river."
Abraham Lincoln (1809-1865)

ABRAHAM LINCOLN had grave doubts about his re-election
to the presidency in the campaign of 1864. Although he
had been unanimously renominated at the Republican
national convention in June, there was some disaffection
in the country over the progress of the war, which was
declared to be a failure by the Democrats, who in August
nominated General George B. McClellan as Lincoln's
opponent.

The great war President's characteristic modesty was
instanced in the course of an address he made on June 9,
1864, to a delegation from the National Union League
who called on him to offer their congratulations on his
renomination. Also in that address he provided a maxim
for following generations of office-holders eager to succeed
themselves in office.

"I do not allow myself to suppose," Lincoln told the
delegation, "that either the convention or the League
have concluded to decide that I am either the greatest or
the best man in America, but rather they have concluded
it is not best to swap horses while crossing the river, and
have further concluded that I am not so poor a horse that
they might not make a botch of it in trying to swap."

Another version, only slightly different in wording,
assigns a date and place of Lincoln's address as other than
those given in the foregoing account.

"This government cannot endure permanently half slave and half free."

Abraham Lincoln

SLAVERY WAS the dominant issue in the 1858 campaign of Abraham Lincoln and Stephen A. Douglas for the latter's seat in the United States Senate, from Illinois. It was in this campaign that the series of brilliant debates between the candidates took place. Lincoln's discussion on the merits of popular sovereignty in the territories, which was inextricably bound with the question of slavery, foreshadowed his speech of acceptance of the Republican nomination for the Senatorship.

In this speech, delivered on June 16, 1858, before the Republican State Convention in Springfield, he said:

" 'A house divided against itself cannot stand.' I believe this government cannot endure permanently half slave and half free. I do not expect the Union to be dissolved. I do not expect the house to fall, but I do expect it will cease to be divided."

* * *

"Say to the seceded States, 'Wayward sisters, depart in peace.' "

Winfield Scott (1786-1866)

BEFORE THE bombardment of Fort Sumter on April 13, 1861, had made civil war inevitable, there were those in the free States who were for allowing the seceding states to withdraw from the Union without a resort to arms.

Among them was General Winfield Scott, in command of the United States Army, who in a letter to William H. Seward, dated March 3, 1861, gave the counsel quoted. Scott was a Virginian but put the Union above sectional loyalties.

"Thenceforward, and forever free."

Abraham Lincoln

ABRAHAM LINCOLN'S Emancipation Proclamation, whereby millions of slaves in the United States were declared free, had long been urged by the radical Republicans. Lincoln, however, was averse to the measure because he believed public opinion was not yet ready for it, and furthermore that it was unwise to issue a proclamation until a victory of the Union forces should precede it, since otherwise it might be considered the drastic recourse of a defeated combatant.

The opportunity he awaited came with the victory of Antietam, and on September 22, 1862, he issued a preliminary order declaring free, effective on January 1, 1863, all slaves in the States which were still in rebellion on that date. The proclamation was issued as a war measure "by virtue of the powers vested in the President as commander-in-chief of the army and navy of the United States." It decreed that "all persons held as slaves within any State, or designated part of a State, the people whereof shall then be in rebellion against the United States, shall be then, and thenceforward, forever free . . ."

The formal Emancipation Proclamation issued on January 1, 1863, confirmed the preliminary act and enumerated the states and sections of states affected by it. In it Lincoln stated that the act was sincerely believed to be one "of justice, warranted by the Constitution, upon military necessity." Formal abolition of slavery in this country was effected by the adoption of the Thirteenth Amendment.

"Government of the people, by the people and for the people."

Abraham Lincoln

THE PERORATION of Lincoln's Gettysburg Address, delivered on November 19, 1863, at the dedication of the battlefield as a soldiers' cemetery, was a call to the American people to dedicate themselves to the perpetuation of the democratic form of government of the nation. Lincoln's words, "that we here highly resolved that government of the people, by the people, and for the people, shall not perish from the earth," were a restatement of the nature of our government made in less rhythmic prose by Daniel Webster in his second speech in the Senate on January 26 and 27, 1830 on the Foote Resolution which led to the celebrated debate with Robert Y. Hayne.

In that speech Webster used the phrase, "The people's Government, made for the people, made by the people, and answerable to the people."

The House of Representatives on April 3, 1918, adopted *The American Creed* formulated by William Tyler Page, which begins, "I believe in the United States of America as a Government of the people, by the people, for the people."

"Now he belongs to the ages."

Edwin McMasters Stanton (1814-1869)

PRESIDENT LINCOLN lay dying in a private house across the street from Ford's Theatre, Washington, where he had been shot in the back of the head by a crazed actor, John Wilkes Booth, as the President and his party sat in a box on the evening of Good Friday, April 14, 1861.

Efforts of the physicians to save the unconscious President's life were unavailing, and Lincoln's wife, members of his family, and his intimates in the government were summoned to his bedside. There as they watched and prayed, the great war President died early in the morning of April 15.

Stanton, Secretary of War, noted for his sternness of character, looked sadly at the lifeless form of his chief. Grief-stricken, with streaming eyes, he pronounced his eulogy of Abraham Lincoln.

* * *

"Seward's Folly."

(1867)

WHEN THE United States in 1867 acquired the colony of Alaska by purchase from Russia the deal was not regarded as a bargain by many people in the country. The price paid, $7,200,000, or about two cents an acre, was held to be an unwise expense on a government with a war debt of nearly $3,000,000,000.

Secretary of State Seward was widely blamed for the transaction. He was ridiculed for buying an "Arctic waste," and Alaska was dubbed his "folly" and his "ice-box."

"Swinging round the circle."

Andrew Johnson (1808-1875)

ANDREW JOHNSON of Tennessee, who became President upon the death of Abraham Lincoln, April 15, 1865, early in his administration incurred the enmity of radical Republicans in the Congress because of the mildness of his reconstruction policies. After several bills providing for drastic treatment of the conquered South had been passed over his veto, Johnson decided to take an active part in the Congressional elections of 1866.

The President left Washington in summer for Chicago where he was to lay the corner stone of the Stephen A. Douglas memorial. His journey there was made by way of a large part of the country, and this circuitous route, which was criticized by James Russell Lowell as "an advertising tour of a policy in want of a party," was described by Johnson himself as "swinging round the circle."

"With malice toward none, with charity for all."

Abraham Lincoln

ABRAHAM LINCOLN was inaugurated for a second term in the presidency in March 1865 at a time when the end of the Civil War was in sight. Grant was relentlessly pressing on toward Richmond and despite General Lee's determined resistance his outnumbered and wearied troops were being steadily pushed back. The fall of the Confederate capital was seen to be imminent.

The President's inaugural address, prophetically it seemed, dealt with the problems that would arise after the great conflict drawing to its close. Characteristic of the magnanimity of his nature and his patriotic statesmanship were the closing words of his address:

"With malice toward none, with charity for all, with firmness in the right as God gives us to see the right, let us strive on to finish the work we are in; to bind up the nation's wounds, to care for him who shall have borne the battle, and for his widow, and for his orphan—to do all which may achieve and cherish a just and lasting peace among ourselves, and with all nations."

His words were a pledge of justice and fair dealing by the Government of the United States for the vanquished South which Lincoln was not destined to be able to keep. Within a few weeks of the day on which the words were uttered the President was dead, the victim of an assassin.

"Hew to the line, let the chips fall where they may."

Roscoe Conkling (1829-1888)

GENERAL ULYSSES S. GRANT was the first of the Presidents to seek a third term in office. After having been elected in 1872 and again in 1876, at the end of his second term he made a two years' tour of the world, and in 1880 was a candidate for renomination to the Presidency.

Roscoe Conkling, United States Senator from New York, noted for his eloquence and his aggressiveness as a leader in the Republican party, was a vigorous advocate of Grant's candidacy, which was quite as vigorously opposed by James G. Blaine of Maine and John Sherman of Ohio, who united in supporting the candidacy of James A. Garfield of Ohio.

Conkling placed Grant's name in nomination at the Republican national convention in Chicago on June 5, 1880, and in his address declared that his candidate, if elected, would "hew to the line of right, let the chips fall where they may." Garfield won the nomination and was elected.

"Turn the rascals out."

Charles Anderson Dana (1819-1897)

HORACE GREELEY, famous editor of the New York *Tribune*, was the candidate of the Liberal Republican Party for President in 1872, running against General U. S. Grant, the regular Republican candidate for re-election. Greeley's campaign was waged on the issue of the necessity for reform in the national administration, which under Grant had been marked by grave scandals, and the cry "Turn the rascals out" was adopted as a party slogan.

The phrase was originated by Charles A. Dana, editor of the New York *Sun*, who had broken with Grant in 1869 and thereafter attacked his administration with exceptional bitterness. Although Dana's antagonism to Grant continued unabated, his support of Greeley's candidacy was not remarkable for any great fervor or force, and Greeley was defeated by Grant.

Dana's slogan for a long time continued to be used derisively to indicate the simulated moral indignation of a party out of power eager to supplant incumbents in office. It is not improbable that the phrase antedated Dana's use of it, for early in the nineteenth century the "spoils" system had become intrenched in party politics, and short terms and rotation in office were advocated by those who desired to provide government jobs for faithful party workers.

"God reigns and the Government at Washington still lives."

James Abram Garfield (1831-1881)

NEWS OF President Lincoln's death early in the morning of April 15, 1865, filled the nation with sorrow and dread. His assassination and the attempts on the lives of others in the government in Washington caused many to believe that they were part of a plot to overthrow the government. Excited throngs in cities throughout the country discussed the effect of Lincoln's death upon the nation.

From a balcony of the United States Customs House in the Wall street district of New York City James A. Garfield, of Ohio, addressed one such throng on the day of the President's death. Garfield, who when President some sixteen years later himself was the victim of an assassin, sought to reassure his hearers that the President's death would not mean the end of the government.

"God reigns and the Government at Washington still lives," he declared.

Garfield had a distinguished military record in the Civil War, having been made a major general in the Union army for gallantry at Chickamauga. At the time of Lincoln's assassination he was a Representative in Congress from Ohio, having resigned his army commission in September 1863.

"The Spirit of '76."

Archibald M. Willard (1836-1918)

PERPETUATION OF the ideals that animated patriots in the American Revolution was the aspiration of many of the men who participated in that struggle and who afterwards were active in the affairs of the young republic. Federalists and Republicans alike invoked the spirit of seventy-six as a guiding influence for the nation. Jefferson in a letter to Monroe, at the time of the enthusiastic receptions to Genet, minister plenipotentiary of France to this country, wrote of "the old spirit of '76" rekindling the newspapers from Boston to Charleston."

Half a century after the adoption of the Declaration of Independence an obscure American painter, himself of Revolutionary stock and a veteran of the Civil War, sought to depict on canvas something of the patriotic fervor of 1776. Archibald M. Willard's picture, "The Spirt of '76," was painted a few months before the opening of the Centennial Exhibition, held in Philadelphia in 1876. It was shown at the Exhibition where it attracted much admiring attention.

It is probably the best known work of an American artist and, regardless of its artistic qualities, it undoubtedly has been inspiring to millions of Americans. It has been reproduced by many processes in countless copies and is so well known as hardly to require description. Willard's father was the model for the central figure of the group of three generations: an old man, bareheaded, his white locks flowing, vigorously beating a drum; a sturdy figure in the uniform of the Continental Army, intently blowing a fife; and a boy in soldier's uniform, also drumming. Behind them is a throng of marching troops, the American flag at their head. The flag showing thirteen stars and the red and white stripes is an anachronism, as this design was not accepted by the Congress until 1777.

Willard's title for the painting originally was "Yankee Doodle," under which name it was shown at the Centennial Exhibition, but subsequently he re-titled it "The Spirit of '76."

*   *   *

"Waving the Bloody Shirt."

Oliver Perry Morton (1823-1877)

FOR YEARS after the close of the Civil War Republican orators made the conflict between the states their favorite subject of campaign speeches. Reviving the spirit of sectionalism, they based their claims to the suffrages of the people upon their loyalty to the Union, as the party that had saved the Union. They laid the responsibility for the war upon the Democratic party and, in general, they fought the war over again on the hustings.

It was in allusion to the frequency with which this issue was used that Oliver P. Morton, United States Senator from New York, referred to the practice as "waving the bloody shirt." The term had been used before in different connections, but Morton's application of it to the use of the Civil War as a campaign issue struck the public as apt and it became popular.

Morton was governor of Indiana during the war, but removed to New York and became Senator from that state in 1867, and associated himself with the Radical wing of the Republican party which had been responsible for the impeachment proceedings against President Andrew Johnson, and opposed a liberal Reconstruction program for the conquered South. He declined President Grant's nomination of him to be minister to Great Britain in 1870, and in 1876 was an unsuccessful candidate for the Republican nomination for President.

"The Plumed Knight."

Robert Green Ingersoll (1833-1899)

ALREADY NOTED as a writer and orator, Robert G. Ingersoll attained nation-wide fame because of his eloquent speech nominating Senator James G. Blaine, of Maine. for the presidency at the Republican national convention in Cincinnati in 1876. In a passage in this speech Ingersoll said of his candidate: "Like an armed warrior, like a plumed knight, James G. Blaine marched down the halls of the American Congress and threw his shining lance full against the brazen forehead of every traitor to his country and every maligner of his fair reputation."

Ingersoll's designation of Blaine as "the plumed knight" was seized upon by Democrats as a term of derision, and by cartoonists as a happy suggestion for caricatures of Blaine. Blaine lost the nomination in 1876 to Rutherford B. Hayes, who was elected. He was again a candidate for the nomination in 1880, and again he lost to James A. Garfield, who won both the nomination and the election. Garfield appointed him Secretary of State, and Blaine during the next four years continued the acknowledged leader of his party, winning the presidential nomination in 1884, but losing the election to Grover Cleveland, the nominee of the Democratic party.

"The Crime of '76."

(1876)

ANOTHER CIVIL war seemed to threaten the country in 1876 as a result of the presidential election in which Rutherford B. Hayes of Ohio was declared winner over his Democratic opponent, Samuel J. Tilden of New York. The voting had been very close, Tilden having received more than a quarter of a million more ballots in the popular voting than Hayes, but the latter received 185 electoral votes to 184 counted for Tilden.

Fraud was charged by both parties, the Democrats asserting that they had carried the Southern States of Louisiana, Florida and South Carolina, which, however, were put in the Hayes column by the Electoral College upon the certification of Republican canvassing boards and governors in the disputed States.

As the controversy increased in bitterness and at times seemed likely to cause a resort to arms, the Congress provided for an Electoral Commission to which the issues were submitted for decision. By the strictly partisan vote of eight Republicans to seven Democrats that body declared on March 2, 1777, two days before the inauguration, Hayes to have won the election by the electoral vote of 185 to 184.

Both parties accepted the decision and an armed conflict was averted, but the Democrats continued to regard the election as having been stolen and for a long time it was referred to by them as "The crime of '76."

"He comes from Appomatox and its famous apple tree."
Charles Graham Halpine (1829-1868)

ONE OF the most ardent supporters of General U. S. Grant
for a third term in the Presidency was Senator Roscoe
Conkling of New York. He had been a powerful advocate
of Grant's policies in his administrations from 1869 to
1877, and when the Civil War hero again became a candidate in 1880, after an absence of four years from the
White House, Conkling vigorously advanced Grant's
claims as against the candidacy of James A. Garfield, his
principal competitor.

Conkling, besides being a skillful politician, was noted
for his oratory and ready wit. When he rose to place
Grant's name in nomination at the Republican national
convention in 1880, there was an air of expectancy in the
convention hall. Pausing a moment for dramatic effect,
Conkling began:

"When asked what state he hails from,
Our sole reply shall be,
He comes from Appomatox
And its famous apple tree."

As Grant's candidacy was based on his war record, the
verse alluding to Grant's victory over Lee, which ended
the Civil War, was appropriate to the theme of the nominating speech. The verse was by Charles G. Halpine, a
veteran of the Civil War in the Union Army, who wrote
under the pseudonym "Private Miles O'Reilly." It had
come to Conkling's notice only the night before he made
his speech.

Halpine, a native of Ireland, had been a newspaper man
in Dublin, Boston and New York before enlisting in the
Sixty-ninth Regiment, New York Volunteers. He served
as the assistant adjutant general in General Hunter's army,
and after the war wrote several books, prose and verse.

"The Solid South."

John Singleton Mosby (1833-1916)

AN AFTERMATH of the Civil War, caused by the experience of the South under carpet-bag rule in the Reconstruction era, was a partisan cohesion of the states that had constituted the Confederacy. Blaming the Abolition sentiment, largely centered in the Republican party, which they considered had been chiefly responsible for bringing on the war between the States, and bitterly resentful of the reconstruction policy imposed upon them by a Republican Congress, the Southern states became as a unit Democratic, as they have since remained, with minor exceptions. They formed the Solid South, a term used by the famous Confederate guerilla and cavalry raider, General John S. Mosby, who in 1876 announced in a letter to a former Confederate comrade that he would support the candidacy of Rutherford B. Hayes, Republican nominee for the presidency. The reason he gave for this was that: "The sectional unity of the Southern people has been the governing idea and bane of their politics," with the result that "every Presidential canvass becomes a battle between the sections."

While it is not certain that the term "Solid South," used by Mosby in this letter, originated with him, the press of the country quickly adopted it as an apt description of the South's political solidarity and generally attributed it to Mosby.

"A Public Office is a Public Trust."

(1884)

PROBABLY NO American President has surpassed Grover Cleveland for industry and painstaking attention to the duties of his high office. With little formal education, no great prestige of family or wealth, and no great gift of oratory or eloquence, he had won political advancement— successively sheriff, mayor, Governor of New York, and now a popular candidate for President of the United States—by the public conviction of his entire sincerity and honesty.

Although he was not the first to voice the sentiment, "A public office is a public trust," his repeated assevera- tions of it in his public papers and addresses and his strict adherence to it as an ideal in the conduct of office served to fix the authorship of the phrase upon him in the mind of the public. Henry Clay in 1829, declared that "Govern- ment is a trust," and in 1872, Charles Sumner wrote: "The phrase, 'public office is a public trust', has of late become common property."

In his letter accepting the Democratic nomination for Governor of New York in October 1882, Cleveland wrote: "Public officers are the servants and agents of the people to execute the laws which the people have made." In his letter accepting the Democratic nomination for President he wrote: "Public officers are the trustees of the people." Finally, in his inaugural address on March 4, 1885, he said: "Your every voter, as surely as your chief magistrate, exercises a public trust."

These repeated declarations of the trusteeship of elected officials, put into a more succinct form, became the motto of the 1884 campaign.

"A Century of Dishonor."

Helen Fiske Hunt Jackson (1830-1885)

THIS COUNTRY's dealings with the Indians from time to time have caused expressions of strong disapproval by humanitarians and lovers of justice and fair dealing. The aborigines of this continent have had no more earnest champion than a woman, Helen Fiske Hunt Jackson, poet, novelist, essayist, and philanthropist.

A native of Massachusetts, she went on a trip to California in 1872 and from there to Colorado where after her marriage she lived the rest of her life. Becoming interested in the Indians as she observed them in the West, she prepared a voluminous report in which she sketched the history of the treatment of the Indians by the government and people of the United States. This document of 457 pages was titled *A Century of Dishonor,* and she sent at her own expense a copy to each member of Congress.

Her appointment as special commissioner to investigate Indian affairs followed, and in 1883 she again reported on their condition. As no betterment of the evils she reported followed, however, she resumed her writings. In her novel *Ramona,* which was published the year before she died, she expressed her indignation at the ill treatment of the Indians by the government of the United States.

"They love him for the enemies he has made."

Edward Stuyvesant Bragg (1827-1912)

GROVER CLEVELAND'S rise in the world of politics was marked by his victories over the machine politicians in his party. As Governor of New York he had won the approval of the better element in all parties, but the attitude of the political bosses toward him was something less than enthusiastic. Dislike of him by practical politicians was intensified as the time of the quadrennial national elections drew near and the name of the Governor of New York was increasingly mentioned for the Democratic nomination for President. The opposition to him came to a head at the Democratic national convention in Chicago in July 1884, known as the Mugwump Convention. Tammany, the New York City Democratic organization, which had its satellites and sympathizers throughout the State, had vigorously opposed Cleveland's candidacy and it controlled the New York delegation at the convention.

It was in allusion to the opposition of Tammany and machine Democrats in general that Edward S. Bragg, chairman of the Wisconsin delegation, in his speech nominating Cleveland on July 9, declared: "They love him for the enemies he has made."

The defiant phrase was caught up and chanted on the convention floor and, with a change of the pronoun "they" to "we," it became a popular cry in the campaign which ended with Cleveland's election.

Bragg was a War Democrat who had fought for the preservation of the Union as commander of the Iron Brigade in many engagements and retired with the rank of Brigadier General of Volunteers. After the war he represented his district in Wisconsin in the Congress.

"Rum, Romanism, and Rebellion."

Samuel Dickinson Burchard (1812-1891)

GROVER CLEVELAND'S election to the Presidency in 1884 was the result largely of an unfortunate remark by a supporter of his Republican opponent, James G. Blaine. The Reverend Dr. Samuel D. Burchard at a reception to Blaine by a delegation of clergymen at the Fifth Avenue Hotel in New York City on October 9, 1884, in an address said: "We are Republicans, and don't propose to have our party identify ourselves with the party whose antecedents have been Rum, Romanism, and Rebellion."

Cleveland's supporters made capital of Blaine's failure to disavow the clergyman's insult to the Catholic Church and the Democratic party, and the alliterative remark undoubtedly cost Blaine many thousands of votes, especially in the crucial state of New York.

* * *

"Ma, Ma, where's my Pa?"

(1884)

IN THE presidential campaign of 1884, with Grover Cleveland, Democrat, running against James G. Blaine, Republican, the latter's campaign managers made public a scandal in Cleveland's early life. It was alleged that as a young man Cleveland was the father of an illegitimate child.

When Cleveland's campaign managers asked him what answer should be made to the charge he replied, "Tell the truth." He admitted that as a young man he acknowledged as his a child born out of wedlock and that he had supported the child. Privately, it was said, he had expressed doubts as to his paternity of the child.

The Democratic candidate's manly course did not save him from more or less criticism and ribald comment, including the chant, "Ma, Ma, where's my Pa?"

To which the reply of Democrats of a kindred strain was, "Gone to the White House, ha, ha, ha."

"If nominated, I will not accept. If elected, I will not serve."

William Tecumseh Sherman (1820-1891)

BETWEEN 1872 and 1884 efforts were made by several leaders in the Republican party to induce General William T. Sherman, of Civil War fame, to become the party's candidate for the Presidency. Sherman, however, refused, and in November 1872, wrote his friend, James S. Rollins, that he would decline "if nominated or elected." As time went on his determination not to be a candidate remained unchanged, and prior to the Republican national convention of 1884, when James G. Blaine attempted to persuade him to change his mind, he again refused. Having in mind the unfortunate experience of his friend, General Grant, in the Presidency, Sherman wrote Blaine that he would be "a fool, a madman, an ass, to embark anew, at sixty-five years of age, in a career that may at any moment become tempest-tossed by the perfidy, the defalcation, the dishonesty or neglect of any one of a hundred thousand subordinates."

Despite this emphatic declaration, the efforts to induce him to become a candidate persisted up to the time of the Republican national convention in Chicago in June 1884. On June 5, John B. Henderson, of Missouri, presiding officer of the convention, wired Sherman in St. Louis that his drafting by the convention was inevitable, that "your name is the only one we can agree upon. You will have to put aside your prejudices and accept the Presidency." Sherman immediately wired his refusal. The wording of the telegram as commonly given differs slightly from that stated by Sherman's son, Thomas, who was present and saw his father's message which he quoted as saying: "I will not accept if nominated, and will not serve if elected."

"Years of almost innocuous desuetude."

[Stephen] Grover Cleveland (1837-1908)

PRESIDENT CLEVELAND and the Senate locked horns early in his first term in the White House. The dispute was over the right of the President to remove holders of federal offices without interference from the Senate. The Democratic party had been successful in the national elections of 1884, which gave the Presidency to a member of that party for the first time since the Civil War, but enough Republicans held over in the Senate to make trouble for the administration.

Cleveland had removed many Republican federal office holders, and the Republican Senators denied his right to do it without "the advice and consent of the Senate," and they demanded that in each case of a removal the President submit to the Senate his reasons for ordering it. In support of their contention the Senators cited the Tenure of Office Act passed during Andrew Johnson's administration as President and used in the effort to impeach Johnson.

Cleveland refused to submit to the Senate his reasons for ordering the removal of office holders, directed administrative departments to withhold such information from the Senate, and in ponderous sentences denied that the Tenure of Office Act, parts of which had been repealed, applied in the instant cases.

In his message of March 1, 1886, to the Senate, referring to the Act, he said:

"After an existence of nearly twenty years of almost innocuous desuetude these laws are brought forth."

The Senate lost in the controversy, and the Tenure of Office Act was repealed on December 17, 1886.

"May God palsy the hand that wrote that order!"

Lucius Fairchild (1831-1896)

THIS DREADFUL curse was hurled at President Cleveland by an officer veteran of the Union Army. It was occasioned by the President's order of May 26, 1887, directing that the captured Confederate regimental flags in the possession of the War Department at Washington be returned to the states of the regiments from which they were captured.

Cleveland's order was issued upon the recommendation of the War Department after an inventory of the trophies, which were packed in boxes. His order, however, was regarded as unfortunate by many of his friends and was violently denounced by his partisan foes, by Union veterans and the Republican press generally.

The most intemperate utterance was that of Lucius Fairchild, of Wisconsin, national commander of the Grand Army of the Republic, who had been a brigadier general of volunteers in the Civil War. Speaking at a meeting of the G.A.R. in Harlem, New York City, he said:

"May God palsy the hand that wrote that order! May God palsy the brain that conceived it, and may God palsy the tongue that dictated it."

President Cleveland revoked the order for the return of the flags on June 15, 1887. Years later President Theodore Roosevelt caused the return of the colors to the former Confederate States without any popular outcry against his act.

"It is a condition which confronts us—not a theory."
[*Stephen*] *Grover Cleveland*

PRESIDENT CLEVELAND, always an advocate of tariff reform, alarmed protectionists within his own party as well as among the Republicans, by his third annual message to the Congress on December 6, 1887. In that message, in view of the advisability of reducing the huge surplus in the national treasury, he urged upon the nation's legislators that the duties on certain manufactured articles of import be reduced and that some of the raw materials of manufacture be admitted duty free.

During 1887 the average rate of tariff on imports was so high that the duties collected totaled more than $55,-000,000 over the requirements for the current expenses of government, but the Congress had refused to revise the tariff imposts.

Arguing the realities of the tariff situation, the President's message said: "Our progress toward a wise conclusion will not be improved by dwelling upon the theories of protection and free trade. . . . It is a condition which confronts us—not a theory."

"This is a billion dollar country."

Thomas Brackett Reed (1839-1902)

As Benjamin Harrison succeeded Grover Cleveland in the Presidency in 1889, his administration had a majority in both houses of the Congress, the first time in fifteen years that this good fortune had befallen the Republican party. Although the majority was a narrow one, it was sufficient, with the aid of the Speaker, Thomas B. Reed, of Maine, to reverse the entire economy policy of the Cleveland administration.

The surplus accumulated under the cautious fiscal policy of Harrison's predecessor was steadily reduced by generous appropriations, which included large sums for coast defenses, lighthouses, harbors, and federal buildings, reimbursements to the State treasuries of direct taxes levied at the beginning of the Civil War, increases in the pension rolls, and the rehabilitation of the Navy.

The opposition of the Democrats was unavailing to halt Congressional spending, and the total of the appropriations of Harrison's first Congress reached $1,000,000,000, a figure astounding in those days. To the Democrats' protests against this "raid on the Treasury," the Speaker, known as "Czar" Reed, calmly replied that "This is a billion dollar country."

"The purification of politics is an iridescent dream."

John James Ingalls (1833-1900)

PERHAPS NO more cynical phrase has been added to the language than the comment made by a politician on the trade of politics. John James Ingalls, United States Senator from Kansas for three terms, was a brilliant orator with a nation-wide reputation as such. His addresses were replete with witty and epigrammatic passages, clever phrases, and at times with withering denunciation.

The cynical phrase by which he is best remembered occurred in an article written by him for the New York *World* in 1890.

"The purification of politics is an iridescent dream," he wrote. "Government is force. . . . The Decalogue and the Golden Rule have no place in a political campaign. The commander who lost the battle through the activity of his moral nature would be the derision and jest of history."

"What are we here for?"

(1894)

CIVIL SERVICE in the United States has had a long, hard, up-hill fight for general recognition. Since the early days of the Republic, American political parties have accepted as entirely valid the dictum that "To the victors belong the spoils," and campaigns have been waged largely with the ultimate goal of providing government jobs for faithful party workers.

This practical view of the principal reason for the existence of political parties was put into the cynical query: "What are we here for?" asked by a delegate to a political convention in Seattle about 1894, when a colleague sought the indorsement by the convention of a civil service proposal for removing several hundred jobs from the control of politics.

The identity of the inquiring delegate has never been established, but his question has endured.

"The crime of 1873."

William Jennings Bryan (1860-1925)

THE SILVER question which was destined to bring about a schism in the Democratic party in 1896 had been agitated for more than two decades prior to that year. Until the outbreak of the Civil War this country had been on a bimetallic basis by law, while most of the nations of Europe were on the gold standard.

In 1873 the United States adopted the gold standard and the coinage laws were revised, causing the silver dollar to be dropped from circulation, although small silver coins and paper currency were in use for convenience. A reaction in favor of silver set in and there was agitation to re-establish the free coinage of silver. This resulted in the enactment of the Sherman Law of 1878, which provided for the purchase monthly of not less than two million dollars' worth nor more than four million dollars' worth of silver. A great influx of silver into the United States ensued.

In August 1892, Representative Richard P. Bland of Missouri introduced in the House a bill providing for the free and unlimited coinage of silver at a fixed ratio to gold. William Jennings Bryan, then serving his second term in the Congress as a representative from Nebraska, took an active part in the debate and in the course of a three-hour speech in the House on August 16 he said:

"Does anyone believe that Mr. Cleveland could have been elected President upon a platform declaring in favor of the unconditional repeal of the Sherman Law? Can we go back to our people and tell them that, after denouncing for twenty years the crime of 1873 we have at last accepted it as a blessing?"

Bryan had supported Grover Cleveland's candidacy for the Presidency, but his speech on this occasion marked a definite parting of the ways of the two Democratic leaders.

"You shall not crucify mankind upon a cross of gold."
William Jennings Bryan

THIS WAS the impassioned close of a speech by Bryan which brought him the presidential nomination at the Democratic National Convention in Chicago, July 7, 1896. Its eloquence stampeded the delegates and Bryan was nominated on the fifth ballot.

The advocates of the free coinage of silver controlled the convention and the leading candidate was Richard P. ("Silver Dick") Bland of Missouri.

Bryan's speech, which was interrupted by cheers and applause at nearly every sentence, closed with the peroration:

"You shall not press down upon the brow of labor this crown of thorns—you shall not crucify mankind upon a cross of gold."

"Sixteen to One."

(1896)

IN THE presidential campaign of 1896 the paramount issue was the free coinage of silver. A revision of the coinage in 1873 put the nation on the gold standard; the silver dollar ceased to circulate and paper currency and small coins were used for convenience.

A reaction in favor of silver set in a few years later, the free coinage of silver was agitated, and in 1878 a compromise law was enacted. This law provided for the purchase of silver bullion in an amount of not less than two million dollars worth monthly nor more than four million dollars worth, but in practice the Treasury bought and coined nothing more than the minimum named.

In 1890 a law was passed for the purchase monthly of 4,500,000 ounces of silver bullion. A great influx of the white metal resulted from these laws and in 1893, the policy of government purchasing of silver was abandoned. Great dissatisfaction in the West, especially among the silver mining interests, followed and the panic of 1893, which had set in before the repeal of the Sherman Law and continued during President Cleveland's administration, was held to be due to the demonetization of silver.

Under the persuasive eloquence of William Jennings Bryan and other advocates of free silver coinage, the Democratic platform of 1896 declared for the free coinage of silver in a fixed ratio. The term "Sixteen to One," which was the ratio named in the platform, became a favorite slogan of the Democrats in the campaign of 1896.

"I am a Democrat still—very still."

David Bennett Hill (1843-1910)

THE NOMINATION of William Jennings Bryan for President in 1896 split the Democratic party. Sound money, or gold, Democrats generally were unable to swallow the free silver doctrine of their party, but some among them who put their political and partisan affiliations above their financial and economic principles remained regular. Some of those who refused to revolt did no more than give passive allegiance to the party and its platform, and in many instances made no effort to conceal their antipathy to the candidate.

David Bennett Hill, of New York, former Lieutenant Governor and Governor of New York, and a staunch organization man who prided himself on his party regularity, was an advocate of sound money who vigorously opposed the free silver heresy embraced by a majority of his party. An unsuccessful aspirant to the presidential nomination in 1892, his boast was, "I am a Democrat."

After Bryan's nomination Hill was quoted in a newspaper interview as declaring, "I am a Democrat still—very still." The inference was rather plain that his attitude in the forthcoming campaign would be one of aloofness. Yet a little later Hill entertained Bryan and Mrs. Bryan at a dinner at his home, Wolfert's Roost. Four years later he seconded Bryan's nomination for President, but declined to be a candidate for the Vice Presidency.

"The enemy's country."

William Jennings Bryan

BRYAN'S IMPASSIONED "Cross of Gold" speech which brought about his nomination for President by the Democratic national convention of 1896 determined the character of the campaign to be waged by his party. It was to be an attack upon the so-called money powers centered in the East, and upon Wall Street so often denounced by the candidate. Bryan had expressed the wish that the formal notification to him of his nomination be made in New York city.

At the railroad station in Lincoln, Nebraska, his home, the nominee prior to setting out for the notification ceremony in Madison Square Garden on August 8, 1896, addressed a crowd that had assembled to bid him godspeed. In this speech he said:

"In ordinary times I would have preferred to have the notification take place at my home. But this is not an ordinary campaign, and, feeling that the principles in which we are interested should rise above any personal preferences which we may have, I have expressed the desire to be notified in New York, in order that our cause might be presented first in the heart of what now seems to be the enemy's country . . ."

His characterization of the East as "the enemy's country" was denounced by his Republican opponents as an appeal to prejudices and an attempt to revive sectional strife that followed the close of the Civil War.

"The Open Door."

John Milton Hay (1838-1905)

THIS COUNTRY'S policy of fairness and friendliness toward China found an able supporter in John M. Hay, Secretary of State under Presidents McKinley and Theodore Roosevelt. While Hay probably was not the first to advocate a hands-off but helpful policy in respect to China, the Open Door formula is so closely associated with his administration of the foreign relations of the United States as to make him seem to be the originator of that policy.

What is known as the Open Door was the international agreement to permit equality of opportunity and freedom of commerce with China, to respect that country's sovereignty and to oppose the cession to foreign powers of Chinese coastal territory.

Hay, in 1899, addressed a note to the great powers, including Japan, proposing that they join in a declaration of the principles of the Open Door, and the proposal was generally accepted. While Japan for a time paid lip-service to this pledge, which she later flagrantly ignored, other countries, especially our own, observed it. Although belatedly, and when our hand was forced by Japan, the United States even went to war in defense of the principles of the Open Door.

Hay was a poet, journalist, historian, and diplomatist. He had been one of Lincoln's private secretaries during the Civil War and was co-author with John G. Nicolay of a life of the great President. After having served in several diplomatic posts, culminating in the ambassadorship to Great Britain, he became Secretary of State in 1898.

"We'll Stand Pat."

Marcus Alonzo Hanna (1837-1904)

PRESIDENT WILLIAM McKINLEY'S campaign for re-election in 1900 was managed by Senator Marcus A. Hanna of Ohio, who had directed the campaign of 1896 in which McKinley defeated William Jennings Bryan, the Democratic candidate. The principal issue in that campaign was the free coinage of silver in a fixed ratio, for which the Democratic platform had declared.

By 1900, however, the silver question seemed to have been shelved, and it was apparent that the Republicans would conduct their campaign for McKinley's re-election upon the record of his administration of the office of President.

That course was indicated by Hanna's reply to a newspaper reporter who had asked him what he considered the issue in the campaign.

"We'll stand pat," Hanna answered, using a poker term that indicates a player's satisfaction with the cards he holds.

"The Full Dinner Pail."

(1900)

IN PRESIDENT MCKINLEY'S first term the Dingley Tariff
Law was enacted, and the benefits to workingmen of the
tariff were emphasized in the 1900 campaign for his re-
election. The depression of 1896 was still fresh in the
minds of voters, and Republican campaign orators omitted
no opportunity to warn them that a repetition of hard
times was probable in the event of McKinley's defeat. In
1896 orders had been placed with factories conditioned
upon Republican success, and in many cases workers had
been told that if Bryan won factories would be closed.

A revival of confidence had followed upon McKinley's
election in 1896, and one of the telling arguments used
by the Republicans in the 1900 campaign was that a continuance of good times, of factories running full time, and
employment at good wages, depended upon the president's
re-election.

The Full Dinner Pail was a much-used campaign slogan,
and the country was flooded with large posters bearing
McKinley's portrait, with the caption "The Advance
Agent of Prosperity." A political cartoon by Grant Hamilton that appeared in *Judge,* a comic weekly, while the
campaign was on, bore the caption "The Full Dinner
Pail."

"Th' Supreme Coort follows th' iliction returns."

Finley Peter Dunne (1867-1936)

McKINLEY'S RE-ELECTION to the Presidency in 1900, was the seal of approval by a majority of the voters upon the course of imperialism which followed upon this country's acquisition of the Philippine Islands as a result of the Spanish-American War. While the Democratic party had fought the presidential campaign on the issue of anti-imperialism, in accepting its defeat it was insistent that, as "the Constitution follows the flag," its benefits must be extended to the peoples of our newly acquired possessions.

The problem of the imperialists, therefore, was that, if the Democrats were right in their contention, the Bill of Rights would add to the difficulties of governing the peoples of dependencies whose peoples were untrained in the ways of democracy. Another and important consideration was that the extension of the Constitution to them would prevent the imposition of tariff duties upon their exports, of which sugar was principal, to the United States.

A series of decisions by the Supreme Court validating the proceedings of the Congress and the administration, which in effect denied to the Philippines "equal rights under the Constitution," was an affirmation of the validity of imperialism policy. These decisions were the occasion of Finley Peter Dunne's ("Mr. Dooley's") shrewd comment: "No matther whether th' Constitution follows th' flag or not, th' Supreme Coort follows th' iliction returns."

Notwithstanding the dictum that the Constitution does not follow the flag, the people of the Philippines under wise and humane administration came to enjoy most of the benefits of the Constitution. Civil government of communities was substituted for military rule, the writ of habeas corpus ran, and popular elections were instituted.

"The little brown brother."

William Howard Taft (1857-1930)

WHEN DEWEY'S fleet destroyed the Spanish fleet in Manila Bay on May 1, 1896, the United States became destined to inherit the Philippine possessions of Spain. Soon after the treaty was signed whereby the islands were ceded to this country, President McKinley appointed as Commissioner to the Philippines, William Howard Taft, of Ohio, former Solicitor General of the United States.

Taft assumed office in 1900, and the wise and humane policy he was to pursue was indicated by his good humored reference to the native Filipino as "The little brown brother."

His kindly gesture of fraternity was not unanimously received with favor either by the natives or by Americans resident in the islands. The armed resistance of Aguinaldo to American dominance of the islands was responsible for this attitude on the part of the Americans. This feeling was whimsically reflected in the lines,

> *"He may be a brother of Big Bill Taft,*
> *But he ain't no brother of mine,"*

in some rhymes by Robert F. Morrison in the *Manila Sunday Times.*

This sentiment found an even more bitter expression in an army song then popular in the islands, one verse of which was:

> *"Damn, damn, damn the Filipino.*
> *Pock-marked khakiac ladrone*;*
> *Underneath the starry flag*
> *Civilize him with a Krag.*
> *And return us to our own beloved home."*

---

* "Copper-colored thief."

Aguinaldo was a Filipino patriot who had led an uprising against the Spanish rulers of the islands in 1896, which resulted, in June 1898, in driving them out with American aid. Aguinaldo became president of the provisional government then formed, but the next year he turned upon his former American allies. After a guerilla war that lasted nearly three years he surrendered and took the oath of allegiance to the American government.

* * *

"Speak softly and carry a big stick."

Theodore Roosevelt (1858-1919)

LESS THAN two weeks before he became President upon the death of President McKinley from an assassin's bullet, Vice President Roosevelt gave an intimation of what as President his foreign policy would be. The occasion was an address at the Minnesota State Fair at Minneapolis on September 2, 1901, in which he said:

"There is a homely adage which runs, 'Speak softly and carry a big stick; you will go far.' If the American nation will speak softly and yet build and keep at a pitch of the highest training a thoroughly efficient navy, the Monroe Doctrine will go far."

"The Big Stick" as a symbol of vigorous official action caught the popular fancy and figured much in contemporary cartoons and comment.

"I took Panama."

Theodore Roosevelt

In 1881 Count Ferdinand de Lesseps, of France, builder of the Suez Canal, began the construction of a canal to pierce the Isthmus of Darien in Colombia to connect the Atlantic and Pacific oceans. Because of extravagance and mismanagement the French company which financed the undertaking went bankrupt and the project was abandoned in 1888.

About the turn of the century Philippe Bunau-Varilla, a French engineer, sought to revive the project and persuaded an American syndicate to acquire the assets of the French Panama Canal Company for the sum of $40,000,000.

President Theodore Roosevelt opened negotiations in 1903 with the government of Colombia, through whose territory the canal would cut, but Colombia's terms were considered exorbitant and negotiations were discontinued.

Bunau-Varilla in the meantime was active in fomenting a revolution whereby Panama would become independent of Colombia and an equitable treaty could be concluded. When two U. S. Army officers who had just returned from the Isthmus, reported to the President that a revolution was imminent, he directed the Navy Department as an emergency measure to station several vessels at various points within easy steaming of the Isthmus.

In the revolution which took place on November 3, 1903, the United States took no active part. The Republic of Panama was proclaimed and was promptly recognized by this country.

Roosevelt had always denied having had a part in instigating or aiding the revolution in Panama. In his memoirs, however, he made the statement:

"I took Panama without consulting the Cabinet."

Also in an interview published in the *New York Times*

March 24, 1911, he said that he had "taken" the Canal Zone and let Congress debate, adding "and while the debate goes on the canal does also."

* * *

"A shorter and more ugly word."

Theodore Roosevelt

THE ILL-FEELING existing between President Theodore Roosevelt and Edward H. Harriman, Wall Street financier, which had its origin in the President's advocacy of regulation of the railroads by the government, reached a climax early in April 1907. It was then that Harriman became a member of Roosevelt's "Ananias Club."

The occasion was the publication on April 2, in a New York newspaper of a letter written by Harriman in December 1905, to Sidney Webster, a friend. In the letter Harriman wrote that in 1904, about a week before the general elections when the chances for the success of the Republican State ticket seemed dubious, he received a request from President Roosevelt that he confer with him in Washington about the political situation in New York.

In compliance with the request, Harriman wrote, he called on the President who told him that the Republican campaign needed money and asked him to help in raising the necessary funds. Harriman agreed, he said, on condition that Chauncey M. Depew of New York be named ambassador to France, to which he asserted the President assented. Harriman then gave his personal check for $50,000 to the New York Republican campaign fund, and raised about $200,000 additional from other sources.

When Harriman's letter appeared Roosevelt promptly denounced it as "a deliberate and willful untruth—by rights it should be characterized by an even shorter and more ugly word."

"The Mysterious Stranger."

John Tinney McCutcheon (1870-   )

IN THE wake of the Civil War came a political alignment
of States that had seceded from the Union. This alignment, known as the Solid South, was a fixed affiliation
with the Democratic party. Although Missouri was not
a Southern State and had not seceded, it had been a slave-
holding State and had been saved to the Union only by
prompt and vigorous action, and politically it was classed
as being of the Solid South.

As Missouri had always voted Democratic in national
elections, great was the astonishment when in 1904, for
the first time since the Civil War, it deserted the Democratic ranks and cast its vote for Theodore Roosevelt, Republican candidate for the Presidency. This defection was
the occasion of a famous cartoon by John T. McCutcheon
that appeared in the Chicago *Tribune* on November 10,
a few days after the election.

McCutcheon's drawing showed two facing ranks, one
representing the Solid South, the other the Republican
party. Between the two ranks was a tall, mustached, frock-
coated figure, with the traditional string tie and Stetson
hat of a Southerner, advancing toward the Republican
ranks. The figure represented Missouri, and on the faces
of those in the ranks of the Solid South as well as of those
in the Republican column amazement and incredulity
were depicted. The caption of the drawing was "The
Mysterious Stranger."

McCutcheon's is one of the outstanding political cartoons of the century and the wording of the caption for
it was used for a fragment by Mark Twain published in
1916

"The Ananias Club."

(1906)

TOWARD THE close of Theodore Roosevelt's tenure of the Presidency the membership of the famous club founded by him had reached respectable numbers, with a "waiting list", as one newspaper commented. Among its most prominent members were Senator Benjamin R. ("Pitchfork Ben") Tillman of South Carolina, and Edward H. Harriman, financier and railroad executive.

The "club" owed its name to the newspaper correspondents in Washington, some of whom were included among those whose veracity had been impugned by the President, who, they said, would talk freely for publication to a newspaper correspondent, but if the public reaction to the published account of the interviewed proved unfavorable he would assert that he had been misquoted or that the correspondent had lied.

This had happened so often that the correspondents, in order to have a witness to the interview in case their truthfulness or accuracy should be questioned adopted the practice of coming in pairs to the White House for the interviews with the President. This is believed to have been the origin of the present established press conferences at the White House.

The occasion for Senator Tillman's nomination to the Ananias Club was his accusation in a debate in the Senate May 12, 1906, on the Hepburn Bill for the regulation of railroads, that Roosevelt had made derogatory remarks about the members of his own party. Tillman was incensed at the President because, he charged, Roosevelt had broken faith with him in ignoring an agreement they had as to certain provisions of the bill.

When Tillman had finished his remarks, Henry Cabot Lodge, of Massachusetts, an intimate of the President, presented a message from Roosevelt which, he said, characterized Tillman's accusation as "a deliberate and unqualified falsehood."

"Perdicaris alive, or Raisuli dead."

John Milton Hay

AN INCIDENT in the war of rebellious subjects against the Sultan of Morocco was brought in dramatic manner to the attention of the Republican national convention in session in Chicago in June 1904. Achmed Ben Mohammed Raisuli, a Moroccan bandit chief, a descendant of the Prophet, was in revolt against the Sultan that year. As a means of making trouble for that ruler, and also of acquiring some needed revenue, he had kidnaped and held for ransom Ion Perdicaris, a native of Greece and a naturalized American.

Raisuli demanded a ransom of $70,000 for the release of Perdicaris, realizing no doubt that the Sultan would be forced by the American government to provide the ransom. The bandit chief furthermore demanded that the Sultan restore to him his property and the honors formerly enjoyed by him.

When the release of Perdicaris was not forthcoming, John Hay, secretary of state, sent a cablegram to the Sultan demanding:

"We want Perdicaris alive, or Raisuli dead."

The terse ultimatum was read from the platform of the convention hall in Chicago and evoked the expected enthusiasm. Roosevelt, who was a candidate for re-election to the Presidency in his own right, did not really need any slogan to arouse the delegates in his favor, being assured of the nomination, but the message to the Sultan probably appealed to his sense of drama. Aside from that the message was effective, for two days later the Sultan paid the ransom price and Perdicaris was released.

The kidnaping of Perdicaris was not Raisuli's first exploit of the kind. He had kidnaped Walter Harris, London *Times* correspondent in Tangier and held him for ransom. Nor was it his last, for in 1907 he held captive

Kaid Sir Harry Maclean, the Sultan's military adviser, the price of whose release was a payment of £20,000 cash, the governorship of the entire Fassi district and other considerable concessions from the Sultan.

            *   *   *

"My spear knows no brother."

Theodore Roosevelt

As PRESIDENT THEODORE ROOSEVELT and Edward H. Harriman continued what was termed "The Roosevelt-Harriman Imbroglio" early in 1907, the President's ire mounted. His release of the correspondence between him and James S. Sherman, chairman of the Republican Congressional Committee, in which he denied Harriman's assertions about his intervention in the New York campaign of 1904, was followed by statements issued from the White House through the Washington newspaper correspondents.

He had discovered, the President declared, the existence of a "rich men's conspiracy" aimed to provide against the continuance of the policy of corporation reform that he had inaugurated. This was to be effected, the President asserted, by naming a "reactionary" for President in 1908. Furthermore, he said, a fund of $5,000,000 had been raised and was available for effectuating this plan.

The President's militant purpose to fight on for his policies, to show no quarter to his political foes, both within and outside the Republican party, was indicated by his statement, "My spear knows no brother."

"Dollar Diplomacy."

(1909)

As SECRETARY OF STATE in the administration of President Taft, Philander C. Knox was noted for his zeal in efforts to promote the employment of American capital abroad. An able lawyer, Knox had been a United States Senator from Pennsylvania and Attorney General of the United States in the administrations of Presidents McKinley and Roosevelt. His activities as Secretary of State in encouraging and protecting American investments in foreign countries won from critics of his foreign policies the contemptuous term "Dollar Diplomacy."

The Secretary's special interest in international finance first became evident in 1909, when he proposed that the railroads in Manchuria be "neutralized," and that Russia, Japan, and other powers join in providing the money whereby China would be enabled to assume ownership of those railroads.

Although this plan fell through because of the refusal of Japan and Russia to accede to it, Knox was successful in having American banks and financial interests participate in making railroad and currency loans to the government of China.

An extension of so-called Dollar Diplomacy to the internal affairs of Nicaragua and Honduras failed, however, when the Senate refused to ratify treaties with the two nations by which their governments would be stabilized through the reorganization of their finances by the government of the United Stattes.

"May every lion do his duty."

(1909)

WHEN THEODORE ROOSEVELT completed his second term in the White House on March 4, 1909, he had no intention of retiring to a life of inactivity. Always an advocate of "the strenuous life", and then little more than fifty years old, he had planned to hunt big game in Africa at the end of his tenure of the Presidency. Another object of the projected expedition was to obtain specimens for the zoological collection of the Smithsonian Institution in Washington.

Accompanied by his twenty-two year old son Kermit, he left New York for Africa on March 23, 1909. The drama that attended most of his movements, as usual attracted much attention throughout the country to his forthcoming big game hunt and the press devoted considerable space to news and comment about it, a favorite quip of paragraphers being, "May every lion do his duty."

The Roosevelt party, however, was well-equipped to cope with the lions of Africa, for besides the customary high-powered rifles and elephant guns, Roosevelt carried a gold-mounted rabbit's foot given to him for good luck by John L. Sullivan, the one-time world champion heavy weight prize fighter. Between the rifles and the luck charm the party during the stay in the Dark Continent killed 512 of Africa's fauna, including seventeen lions and a varied assortment of feral animals consisting of rhinos, elephants, hippopotami, giraffes, gazelles, hyenas, and others with names unfamiliar to the average American.

Upon emerging from Africa Roosevelt visited Rome, Paris, Berlin, Christiania, Oxford and London, returning to the United States in June 1910.

"My hat is in the ring."

Theodore Roosevelt

As THE rift widened between President Taft and his friend and predecessor in office, public interest in the question whether Roosevelt would be a candidate for the Republican nomination for President became intense at the beginning of 1912. An open break with Taft, succeeding ever more strained relations between the two one-time friends, was caused in November of the year preceding when the Attorney General filed a suit of dissolution against the United States Steel Corporation.

The Attorney General alleged that the corporation was a monopoly which had been achieved through its purchase of the Tennessee Coal and Iron Company four years before, and that in acquiring the property the steel corporation had misled Roosevelt, who was then President.

This infuriated Roosevelt, who angrily denied that he had been misled. Roosevelt's criticism of Taft and his unconcealed dissatisfaction with his administration was followed in January 1912, by a round robin signed by seven governors of progressive states, urging him to be a candidate for the Presidency.

His answer came informally late in February when at the railway station in Cincinnati, on his return from a Republican state convention in Columbus, Ohio, he was asked whether he would run for the Presidency.

"My hat is in the ring", he replied, adding: "The fight is on and I am stripped to the buff."

More formally, on February 24, he announced his candidacy in a letter to the seven governors in which he stated: "I will accept the nomination for the Presidency if it is tendered to me."

"We stand at Armageddon, and we battle for the Lord."
                                        Theodore Roosevelt

ON THE eve of the Republican national convention which
opened on June 18, 1912, in Chicago, Roosevelt addressed
a great throng in the Auditorium. In the peroration of
his speech he said:

"We fight in honorable fashion for the good of mankind; fearless of the future, unheeding of our individual
fates, with unflinching hearts and undimmed eyes; we
stand at Armageddon, and we battle for the Lord."

He failed to get the Republican nomination for President, for the Taft delegates controlled the convention and
they unseated seventy-two Roosevelt delegates in favor of
his adversary's delegates.

At the close of the convention Roosevelt announced
the formation of the new Progressive party, and two
months later was nominated as its candidate for the Presidency.

"Would that we could do something . . . to knock Mr. Bryan into a cocked hat."

[*Thomas*] *Woodrow Wilson (1856-1924)*

AN ECHO of the split in the Democratic party over the silver question in 1896 reverberated in 1912 to plague Woodrow Wilson, then an avowed candidate for the Democratic nomination for President. Although the free coinage of silver by this time had long ceased to be an issue, William Jennings Bryan, who had been its foremost advocate, was still a power in the counsels of the party and he was known to be friendly to Wilson's ambition.

Wilson, then governor of New Jersey, was to be the principal speaker at the Jackson Day dinner to be held in New York early in January, and Bryan was to be one of the distinguished guests of the occasion which was to serve for the formal launching of the Wilson candidacy. A few days before the dinner a letter from Wilson to Adrian Joline, New York lawyer and Princeton alumnus, was published. In this letter the writer expressed the wish:

"Would that we could do something, at once dignified and effective, to knock Mr. Bryan into a cocked hat."

The letter was dated April 29, 1907, when Wilson was president of Princeton University. Its genuineness was not denied by Wilson, however much it must have embarrassed him to have it made public years after the issue that had prompted it no longer existed.

Whatever the purpose in bringing it to light, the letter was of no effect in causing a rift between Wilson and Bryan. Wilson began his speech with a handsome tribute to Bryan. Upon his election to the presidency he named Bryan Secretary of State.

"They've gotta quit kickin' my dawg aroun'."

(1912)

AT THE historic Democratic national convention in Baltimore in June 1912, at which Champ Clark, of Missouri, Speaker of the House in the Congress, vainly sought the nomination for President, a rustic campaign song adopted by his followers was frequently heard. One verse of the song ran:

> *Ev'ry time I come to town*
> *The boys keep kickin' my dawg aroun';*
> *Makes no dif'rence if he is a houn'.*
> *They've gotta quit kickin' my dawg aroun'.*

The song was supposed to indicate the wide difference between the two principal aspirants to the nomination, the homespun humanity of Clark contrasted to the cold professional austerity of Woodrow Wilson, his principal rival for the nomination. Clark's home town in Missouri was far distant from the hill country of the Ozarks where "houn' dawgs" abound, but the song nevertheless was considered appropriate for a candidate from whatever part of Missouri.

"Watchful Waiting."

(1913)

A "MEXICAN QUESTION" awaited solution when Woodrow Wilson took office as President of the United States in 1913. The long rule of Porfirio Diaz as president and dictator of the Mexican republic had been ended in 1911 by a revolt headed by Francisco Madero, who became President of Mexico. Madero was assassinated in 1913 in a counter revolt led by Victoriano Huerta, who became Provisional President. The Mexican situation was further complicated when early in 1914 Venustiano Carranza and Francisco (Pancho) Villa took the field against Huerta. The Wilson administration was thus confronted at the outset by a civil war in the country on our southern border, in which the guerilla warfare of rival chieftains kept the country along the Rio Grande in a constant state of turmoil. There were about 75,000 Americans residing in Mexico and more than a billion dollars of American capital was invested in that country, especially in oil properties.

Wilson steadfastly refused either to recognize the Huerta government or to intervene in the quarrel between him and Carranza. This policy of "watchful waiting," as it came to be known, was interrupted in April 1914, when in reprisal for an insult to the flag by the Huerta government, the United States occupied Vera Cruz temporarily. Thereafter a force of American troops was stationed along the Rio Grande for the maintenance of order, and watchful waiting was resumed until the restoration of constitutional government in 1920.

"To reward deserving Democrats."

William Jennings Bryan

As SECRETARY OF STATE in President Wilson's first administration, William Jennings Bryan was not so much absorbed in foreign policies as to ignore the solicitations of office-seekers. That he believed that "to the victors belong the spoils" would seem to be apparent from a letter he addressed to Walter W. Vick, Receiver General of Customs in Santo Domingo, on August 20, 1913.

In the letter the Secretary wrote: "Can you let me know what positions you have at your disposal with which to reward deserving Democrats?"

Bryan's appeal for aid to the members of his party was widely criticized, but he professed to see nothing improper in it. In an interview published in the New York *Times* January 16, 1915, he was quoted as saying: "I am glad to have the public know that I appreciated services of those who work in politics and feel an interest in seeing them rewarded."

"There is nothing final between friends."

William Jennings Bryan

A CRISIS in the relations between the United States and Japan was caused by the passage in April 1914, by the California legislature of an act excluding Japanese from holding title to real estate in that state. The measure was considered in Japan to be an affront to the dignity of that nation, and great resentment was expressed in the Japanese press. Although California's right to enact such legislation was not questioned, President Wilson saw in it a threat to peace between the two nations and in an effort to preserve friendly relations he requested Secretary of State Bryan to go to California and endeavor to effect some arrangement by which the Japanese would be mollified.

Bryan addressed the California legislature and succeeded in obtaining its consent to work out any plan that would save Japanese "face" while still protecting the state from undue competition of foreign labor. This agreement in principle, however, did not satisfy Japan's wounded pride and that country's Ambassador in Washington, Viscount Chinda, late in May called on the Secretary of State to protest formally in the name of his government against the act as an indignity to his country and its people. Bryan explained the peculiar situation in California and diplomatically sought to show his caller that the legislation was an economic measure without intent to offend Japanese sense of honor. The explanation failed to satisfy the Ambassador and after the conversation had lasted some time Chinda asked Bryan directly if the California law would stand. When the Secretary answered in the affirmative, Chinda arose to take his leave, remarking:

"I suppose, Mr. Secretary, this decision is final."

"There is nothing final between friends", Bryan answered, grasping the Ambassador's hand.

The conversation was resumed, and resulted in the agreement upon a statement phrased to assuage the anger and hurt of the Japanese people and their government.

* * *

"He Kept Us Out of War."

(1916)

THE CENTRAL theme of the address of the chairman at the Democratic national convention on June 7, 1916, was that President Wilson's statesmanship had saved this country from being drawn into the first World War, then at its height. The campaign for Wilson's re-election was waged mainly on the issue of the President's defense of American rights against their violation by the belligerents, especially Germany, and the cry, "He kept us out of war", heard at the convention, became a popular campaign slogan.

Early in the year Wilson had scored two notable successes in his policy in meeting problems created by the war. He had caused the defeat of a resolution in the Congress to forbid American citizens to travel on armed belligerent ships, which Germany had threatened to sink without warning. Also he had forced the German government to promise that merchant ships would not be destroyed "without warning and without saving human lives." This had been brought about by the President's threat to the Kaiser to sever diplomatic relations with the German Government after the French steamer *Sussex* had been sunk by a German submarine.

"America First."

[*Thomas*] *Woodrow Wilson*

ALMOST FROM the beginning of World War I there was evident the belief that the United States either would be drawn into it or should voluntarily enter it upon the side of the Allies. Opponents of the administration condemned what they considered the President's pacifism and favored American participation in the war against the Central Powers. Many citizens of alien origin, whose sympathies were with the Germans, or who were anti-British, engaged in active propaganda to sway American sentiment in favor of Germany and its allies. Nor was propaganda in support of the Allied Powers lacking.

On April 20, 1915, President Wilson addressed the annual meeting of the Associated Press in New York City. Referring briefly to the war and our own state of neutrality, he asked if it were "not likely that the nations of the world will some day turn to us for the cooler assessments of the elements engaged?" He declared that we must make up our minds what are the best things to do, and what are the best ways to do them. He said that "our whole duty, for the present, at any rate, is summed up in the motto, 'America first.' Let us think of America before we think of Europe, in order that America may be fit to be Europe's friend when the day of tested friendship comes. The test of friendship is not now sympathy with the one side or the other, but getting ready to help both sides when the struggle is over."

The intense nationalism of the address, which became the subject both of praise and criticism, was emphasized by Wilson's closing sentence: "I am not sure that I am worthy to represent you, but I do claim this degree of worthiness—that before everything else I love America."

Daniel Webster in his speech at the laying of the corner stone of the Bunker Hill monument in Charlestown,

Mass., June 17, 1825, foreshadowed Wilson's patrotic sentiment in the sentence: "Let our object be, Our Country, Our Whole Country, and Nothing but Our Country."

*   *   *

"All dressed up, with nowhere to go."

William Allen White (1868-1944)

THEODORE ROOSEVELT for the second time was nominated for the Presidency by the Progressive Party in June 1916. The nominee of the Republican Party was Charles Evans Hughes. After conferences extending over several weeks Roosevelt endorsed the Hughes' candidacy, thereby eliminating himself from the presidential race.

His refusal to run meant the virtual dissolution of the Progressive Party and was a great disappointment to most of its members, especially to William Allen White, editor of the Emporia (Kansas) *Gazette*, who had taken a leading part in drafting the Progressive platform, and in commenting on his leader's defection he complained that the members of the Progressive Party had been left "all dressed up in their fighting clothes, with nowhere to go."

"The President cannot be disturbed."

　　　　　　　　Charles Evans Hughes, Jr. (1889-　　　)

ON ELECTION night in November 1916 both presidential candidates, President Wilson and Charles Evans Hughes, former associate justice of the United States Supreme Court, retired early. Both believed that the result of the election was a Republican victory, and they had good reason for so believing. The early returns of the balloting throughout the country had shown a heavy vote against the re-election of President Wilson, and before nine o'clock that evening many newspapers throughout the East, including the New York *Times* and the New York *World,* had conceded the election of Hughes.

Later returns, however, put the election in doubt, with the unreported California vote probably the deciding factor. As there had been great disaffection among the Republicans of that state, due to a supposed slight by Mr. Hughes to an influential Republican leader there, it was considered not unlikely that the state would go Democratic.

A short time after midnight a reporter of a New York newspaper called Mr. Hughes' hotel to tell him that the California result was in doubt. A voice, said to have been that of young Charles E. Hughes, Jr., answered.

"The President cannot be disturbed," he told the reporter.

The latter was insistent in his request to be allowed to speak to Mr. Hughes.

"You will have to come back in the morning," he was told. "The President cannot be disturbed."

"Well when he wakes up, just tell him he isn't President," the caller retorted.

The reporter's prediction was not actually verified until the second morning after the election.

"He [Theodore Roosevelt] was a walking day of judgment."

John Burroughs (1837-1921)

LESS THAN a year before his death John Burroughs, the naturalist and essayist, in a striking phrase summed up his estimate of a phase of the character of Theodore Roosevelt. The two men had been intimate friends, drawn closer together by the love of nature they had in common.

Burroughs admired Roosevelt, not only for his interest in the things of nature and his love of the outdoors, but also for his qualities of statesmanship, his activities in the cause of reform in government, and his bold attacks upon what he considered to be public evils.

Speaking of his friend, who had recently died, the naturalist was quoted in an article published in *Forest and Stream,* January 1928, as saying:

"He had a genuine love of nature and he knew nature, too, and in this field he might have been as great as he was in his dearer field of public life, in which he was a walking day of judgment."

"A little group of wilful men."

[*Thomas*] *Woodrow Wilson*

As WOODROW WILSON'S first term in the Presidency drew to its close all his efforts to avert this country's entrance into the World War seemed destined to be unavailing. The German Ambassador, Count von Bernstorff, on January 31, 1917, formally notified the State Department in Washington that his government had withdrawn its pledge of 1916 and that unrestricted submarine warfare would be resumed on the following day. As this meant that American merchant vessels would be subject to attack and sinking by German U-boats without warning, and that American lives would be in danger in the naval war zone defined by Germany, von Bernstorff was promptly dismissed by the United States Government.

Subsequently two American merchant vessels were sunk by German submarines, and on February 26, the President appeared before the Congress and requested authorization to arm American merchant ships. On March 1, the House passed a bill granting this authority. The bill was referred to the Senate Foreign Relations Committee, of which William J. Stone of Missouri was chairman, and he immediately set about to prevent the passage of the measure. In this he was joined by a group of ten Republican Senators, the more prominent of whom were Robert M. LaFollette, of Wisconsin, Henry Cabot Lodge, of Massachusetts, and Boies Penrose, of Pennsylvania, who started a successful filibuster to prevent the passage of the bill before the expiration of the session of the Congress on March 4. When the two houses adjourned *sine die* on that date seventy-five Senators signed a statement declaring they favored the enactment of the pending measure and would have voted for its passage had not the filibuster prevented it from coming to a vote. The President was indignant at this frustration of the will of the majority by a few men, and he issued a statement condemning the rules of the Senate which made it possible and declaring that "a little group of wilful men, representing no opinion but their own," had rendered the government "helpless and contemptible."

* * *

"The hyphenated American always hoists the American flag undermost."

Theodore Roosevelt

LONG BEFORE the dangers of "fifth columns" had been demonstrated by the experiences of various countries during the era of Nazi-controlled Germany, American citizens of divided loyalties were objects of severe criticism in this country. Woodrow Wilson and Theodore Roosevelt both deplored such unpatriotic attitudes. President Wilson soon after his inauguration for his first term delivered an address in Washington on May 16, 1914, condemning what has come to be known as "hyphenism". The occasion was the unveiling of a statue of Commodore John Barry, by some of his historian admirers regarded as the "Father of the American Navy."

"John Barry," said the President, "was an Irishman, but his heart crossed the Atlantic with him. He did not leave it in Ireland. . . . Some Americans need hyphens in their names because only part of them has come over."

In the light of the bitter partisanship of those Americans expressing sympathy with one side or the other in World War I, the President's reproof seems mild.

Theodore Roosevelt, a consistent foe of diluted Americanism, as former President employed terms more vigorous and downright in expressing his aversion to it. In his book *Fear God and Take Your Own Part* he wrote:

"The hyphenated American always hoists the American flag undermost."

"There is no right to strike against the public peace by anybody, anywhere, any time."

Calvin Coolidge (1872-1933)

OVERNIGHT CALVIN COOLIDGE, Governor of Massachusetts, became a national figure because of the publicity given to a ringing utterance by him. The police of Boston, who had been organized as a local of the American Federation of Labor, went on strike in September 1919, and for several days the city was without police protection and at the mercy of lawless elements. Edwin W. Curtis, Boston Police Commissioner, invoked the aid of Governor Coolidge in the emergency and State troops were sent to Boston to protect its citizens. The action aroused organized labor and Samuel Gompers, president of the American Federation of Labor, hastened to Boston to take charge of the strike.

Voicing the objection of organized labor to the presence of troops Gompers on September 14, sent a telegram to the Governor asking for the removal from office of Commissioner Curtis. Promptly the Governor replied by telegram to Gompers, denying his request, upholding Curtis, and declaring: "There is no right to strike against the public peace by anybody, anywhere, any time." The striking phrase caught the public fancy, was indorsed generally, and helped measurably to bring about Coolidge's nomination as Vice President by the Republican party in 1920.

"We must stabilize and strive for normalcy."
Warren Gamaliel Harding (1865-1923)

IN THE presidential campaign of 1920 the dominant note of Republican speeches was the need for a return to practical thinking after the idealism of President Wilson's two administrations. This thought was expressed in the speech of Senator Warren G. Harding of Ohio on July 22 in accepting the Republican presidential nomination. On that occasion he declared that "We must stabilize and strive for normalcy."

His use of the word "normalcy", instead of the usual term "normality", in the sense of the *status quo ante,* attracted almost as much attention and comment by the press as the actual substance of his speech, although he had used it in prior speeches in the pre-convention campaign. In an address before the Ohio Society of New York on January 20, 1920, he referred to "a sane normalcy," and on May 19 that same year in an address in Boston he declared: "America's present need is not heroics but healing, not nostrums but normalcy." His fondness for the word had the effect, for a time at least, of removing it from the limitation of a technical term in mathematics.

"In a smoke-filled room in some hotel."

Harry Micajah Daugherty (1860-1941)

EVENTS OF the Republican national convention that met
in Chicago in June 1920, were accurately foretold by one
of the principal actors in it. The candidates for the Presidency whose names were prominently before the delegates
were Senator Warren Gamaliel Harding of Ohio, Senator Hiram Johnson of California, Frank O. Lowden of
Illinois, and General Leonard Wood of New Hampshire.

The progressive element among the delegates, led by
Senator William E. Borah of Idaho, favored the nomination of Johnson. On the first ballot Harding received only
651½ votes and seemed to be losing. As Johnson's strength
grew weaker in subsequent ballotting Borah announced
that if either Wood or Lowden were nominated the pro-
gressives would bolt the convention. The convention re-
cessed at the end of the first day's ballotting, badly dead-
locked.

Harry M. Daugherty, an Ohio politician who was Harding's manager at the convention, in an interview in the
New York Times had said: "The convention will be dead-
locked, and after the other candidates have gone their
limit, some twelve or fifteen men, worn out and bleary-
eyed for lack of sleep will sit down about two o'clock in
the morning around a table in a smoke-filled room in
some hotel and decide the nomination. When that time
comes, Harding will be selected."

It was as Daugherty had foretold. Early in the morning
following the dead-locked session Senator Henry Cabot
Lodge of Massachusetts and others of the so-called "Senate
oligarchy" met in the room of George Harvey in the
Blackstone Hotel to review the situation and arrive, if
possible, at an agreement on the candidate to be nominated. During the meeting they were in touch by tele-
phone with Senator Boies Penrose of Pennsylvania at his

home. When the meeting broke up they had decided on the candidate. Harding was nominated that day on the tenth ballot, his final vote being 692½ votes.

"The smoke-filled room" since then has been the tag of political machine-made decisions.

*   *   *

"Keep Cool With Coolidge."

(1924)

TACITURNITY AND calm were notable characteristics of President Calvin Coolidge's personality. As successor to President Harding upon the latter's death in August 1923, Coolidge's administration was marked by his adherence to his predecessor's policy of "normalcy." During the two years before Harding's death Republican disaffection with the party organization developed and in 1922 the Republican majority in the House was materially reduced in the Congressional elections. The dissatisfaction of farmers, especially in the West, resulted in the formation of an agricultural bloc in the Congress, and a short time before Harding died a third party movement threatened.

The unrest and political turmoil failed to disturb Coolidge's habitual calm and placidity, and when he was nominated for the Presidency by the Republican national convention in 1924 the campaign slogan, "Keep Cool With Coolidge", was adopted.

"The Kiss of Death."

Alfred Emanuel Smith (1873-1944)

FOR FOURTEEN years the politics of New York State were enlivened by the bitter political enmity between Alfred E. Smith and William Randolph Hearst. Prior to 1922 the two men had been political foes, but in that year their rivalry reached a climax of bitterness. While Smith's political fortunes had progressed almost without check, Hearst had been unsuccessful, except for a term as representative in Congress, in his quest for political preferment.

In 1922 Smith was the Democratic choice for the gubernatorial nomination, and Hearst was an aspirant to a seat in the Senate from New York. The editor had obtained the assent of the head of Tammany, Charles F. Murphy, to his candidacy, but Smith resolutely refused to consent to run on the same ticket with Hearst. For hours Murphy pleaded with Smith to agree to Hearst's nomination by the Democrats for Senator, but Smith was obdurate, and Murphy at length was forced to yield.

This was Hearst's final effort to obtain political office, and the frustration of his ambition by Smith was the unforgiveable offense. His attacks on Smith in his newspapers were resumed and were frequent and unrestrained.

Smith was a candidate for re-election to the governorship in 1926. When he learned that Hearst was supporting Ogden L. Mills, Republican, to oppose him, he exclaimed delightedly:

"It is the kiss of death!"

Mills was defeated, and Smith was re-elected to a fourth term as Governor of New York.

"I do not choose to run for President."
Calvin Coolidge

As ALWAYS when the end of a President's term is in sight, public interest was keen in 1927 as to whether President Calvin Coolidge would be a candidate to succeed himself in the White House. It was conceded that the nomination would be his if he desired it. Markedly taciturn and prone to keep his own counsel, the President had not done or said anything to indicate his probable course.

Not until August 1927, did he give any inkling of his attitude, and then only after his own fashion. He had gone that summer to the Black Hills for his vacation and a "temporary White House" had been established in Rapid City, South Dakota. Here on August 2 he summoned the newspaper correspondents assigned to "cover" the President and handed them a typed statement, which read:

"I do not choose to run for President in 1928."

That was the extent of the statement, and the President then and thereafter refused to elaborate or explain it. Somewhat less than unequivocal, it left both the press and public puzzled. Did it mean that, while he would not of his own choice seek the nomination, he would not refuse it if he were "drafted?" Or was his meaning that, although he would not "run in 1928," he would be receptive to a nomination four years later? Like Theodore Roosevelt, Coolidge had succeeded to the Presidency upon the death of the incumbent in that office. Like Roosevelt, he had been elected President subsequently in his own right. Roosevelt after an interval of four years out of office had sought re-election in 1912.

The ambiguity which was generally read into his statement was unofficially explained in many varying ways. One which, in the absence of any from the President himself, was widely accepted was that the word "choose", in the idiom of New England, indicates a definite decision.

"A Chicken in Every Pot, a Car in Every Garage."

(1928)

IN THE presidential campaign of 1928 the issues presented no sharp differences as between the Republican and Democratic parties. The candidates, Herbert C. Hoover, Republican, and Alfred E. Smith, Democrat, were pretty well agreed on the tariff question, traditionally the point of difference between the two parties, and the record in office of both men was excellent. As the candidate of the party in power, Hoover had a considerable advantage. Additionally, the "Coolidge Boom" was still in full swing and there seemed to be no limit to the prevailing prosperity.

The character of the campaign to be conducted by the Republicans was foreshadowed in their candidate's speech accepting the nomination. "We in America today are nearer to the final triumph over poverty than ever before in the history of a land," he declared. He further asserted that "the poorhouse is vanishing from among us," and that, while the nation had not yet reached the goal, if it went forward with the policies of the eight years just passed, it would soon be within sight of the day when poverty would be banished from the land.

Republican "literature" in this campaign provided the Democrats with material which they used in 1932 with greater effect than in 1928 when the advertisement sponsored by the Republican National Committee which appeared in newspapers of October 20, 1928, asserted that Republican prosperity had reduced hours and increased earning capacity, and had put "a chicken in every pot and a car in every garage." This boast, borrowed from Henri IV of France, whose aspiration was for a fowl in the pot of every peasant in the land on Sundays, was repeated derisively by Democratic orators and it was popularly, and mistakenly, attributed to one of Hoover's campaign speeches.

The nearest approach to it by him, however, was in the campaign speech delivered in Madison Square Garden on October 22, in which he said: "The slogan of progress is changing from the full dinner pail to the full garage."

* * *

"The happy warrior, Alfred Smith."

Franklin Delano Roosevelt (1882-1945)

LONG AFTER Alfred E. Smith's political career had ended, and until his death, he was known as the Happy Warrior, the title conferred on him by his warm friend and admirer, Franklin D. Roosevelt. Even after an impairment of their intimacy had developed, Smith continued to bear the designation given him by his friend.

In the 1928 Democratic National Convention in Houston, Texas, at which Smith was the leading candidate for the Presidential nomination, Roosevelt made the principal speech placing his name in nomination. At the climax of his address he said: "We offer one who has the will to win—who not only deserves success but commands it. Victory is his habit—the happy warrior, Alfred Smith."

Smith won the nomination, but lost the election to Herbert Hoover. The phrase used by Roosevelt occurs in the title of Wordsworth's poem, "The Character of the Happy Warrior." Its more recent use before that by Roosevelt was in a eulogy of Grover Cleveland at the time of his death in 1908.

"Let's look at the record."

Alfred Emanuel Smith

IN HIS many political speeches Alfred E. Smith depended mainly on the logic of facts for the strength of his argument. In his long public life, in which he had been successively a member of the New York State Assembly, Sheriff of New York County, President of the New York City Board of Aldermen, four times Governor of the State of New York, and nominee of the Democratic party for President, Smith had ample opportunities for his political education.

His speeches were never attempts at flights of rhetoric, but were replete with common sense and homely wit and humor and they usually contained some quotable expression which gained popular currency. They were marked by clarity and simplicity of expression and he sought to buttress his arguments with data which were of record. It was his practice when delivering a speech dealing with controversial subjects to have with him envelopes marked with the topics of discussion and containing newspaper clippings and memoranda bearing on the topics.

When refuting some assertion, or in support of his own, he would resort to one of the envelopes and with the prefatory remark, "Let's look at the record," he would read from the contents of the envelope. This method of corroborating his own statements was usually effective with his audiences.

Of Smith's familiarity with statistics and his ability to understand and interpret them, Robert Moses, of New York, said: "He could make statistics sit up, beg, roll over, and bark."

"Sons of the Wild Jackass."

George Higgins Moses (1869-1944)

THE SPIRIT of insurgency among members of the Republican party, which was rampant in the days of the Progressive party of Theodore Roosevelt, had not been entirely laid even by the time Herbert Hoover became President in 1929. The protests of Republicans against the reactionary tendencies of the leaders of their party were particularly vehement in the South and West, and their discontents were echoed by their Senators and Representatives in the Congress.

Senator George H. Moses of New Hampshire, who was permanent chairman of the national convention at which Hoover was nominated for the Presidency, was also chairman of the Republican Senatorial Campaign Committee. A leader in the conservative wing of his party, he was a brilliant speaker whose oratory was marked by a biting wit and independent utterances. After the election of Hoover, in condemning the radicalism of the Western and Southern Senators in his party, Moses referred to them as "Sons of the wild jackass." The epithet, however amusing to others, was strongly resented by progressive Republicans and almost split the party. Moses, however, refused to retract his characterization of them.

Moses, who was Senator from New Hampshire from 1918 to 1932, had been United States Minister to Greece and Montenegro from 1909 to 1912.

"The Brains Trust."

James M. Kieran (1901-   )

EVEN BEFORE Franklin D. Roosevelt was elected President for his first term the circle of his intimate advisers had been christened with a collective name. The coteries of trusted presidential advisers, who for the most part were not office holders, and who in preceding administrations had been known variously as "The Kitchen Cabinet", the "Tennis Cabinet", or the like, in President Franklin D. Roosevelt's administration became known as "The Brain Trust."

The origin of the term, which the public promptly adopted with a slight change, has been generally attributed to James M. Kieran, a New York newspaperman. However, Allen White used the title "The Brain Trust" for an article in the *Saturday Evening Post* of March 21, 1903. Mr. Kieran in the course of an interview with Mr. Roosevelt at his Hyde Park home in August 1932, alluded to the group of college professors who were known to have aided the candidate in the preparation of his campaign speeches as "The Brains Trust."

The phrase caught on with the newspapers and the public and has persisted even through many changes in the personnel of the President's circle of advisers. The most prominent of the original circle included Raymond Moley and Rexford Tugwell, of Columbia University, New York; Charles Taussig of Harvard University; General Hugh Johnson, Adolf Berle and others who figured in the public mind as intellectuals.

In the course of time many shifts in Roosevelt's personnel occurred, so that at the time of his death few of the original members of the Brain Trust had any connection with his administration.

"As Maine goes, so goes the country."

(1888)

IN PRESIDENTIAL elections from 1860 to 1888 the Republican party had been victorious, except in a single instance, 1884, when the Democratic candidate, Grover Cleveland, was elected President. When the Republican candidate, Benjamin Harrison, was elected in 1888, the phrase, "As Maine goes, so goes the country", was adopted as a political maxim. It originated in the fact that in Maine state elections were held several weeks in advance of the national elections. As the state ballotting there invariably resulted in the election of Republicans, and as the Republican party was successful in eight out of eleven national elections, from 1888 to 1928, the result in Maine was generally accepted as foreshadowing the outcome in the national election following.

This tradition was shattered, however, by the overwhelming victory in 1932 for Franklin D. Roosevelt over Herbert C. Hoover, Republican candidate for re-election. Four years later Alfred M. Landon, of Kansas, the Republican candidate for President, was defeated by Roosevelt who won the electoral votes of every state except Maine and Vermont. Commenting on this crushing defeat, James A. Farley, of New York, Roosevelt's campaign manager, said, "As Maine goes, so goes Vermont."

"The grass will grow in the streets of a hundred cities."
Herbert Clark Hoover (1874-   )

THE INDUSTRIAL depression which began in 1929, late in
the first year of President Hoover's administration, lasted
throughout his term and approached a climax as his tenure of office drew to its close. There was an almost unanimous lack of confidence among business men, factories and
mills were closed down, mortgages on farms and homes
were foreclosed, banks were failing in great numbers, federal, state and local taxes were high, the public debt had
increased enormously, the Government was living a hand-
to-mouth existence and "Hoover Towns," groups of miserable shacks housing unemployed and homeless men,
dotted the landscape throughout the country. Against this
dismal background Hoover's campaign for re-election was
conducted in 1932.

The President had made four tours of the West, as-
suring his hearers that the worst was over and prosperity
was ahead of the country, when he came to New York
City to make his final speech of the campaign in Madison
Square Garden on October 31, 1932. In the course of that
address he spoke of the importance to American business
and labor of a protective tariff, whose retention would be
assured by the return of the Republicans to power. In this
connection he said:

"Whole towns, communities and forms of agriculture
with their homes, schools and churches have been built
up under this system of protection. The grass will grow
in the streets of a hundred cities, a thousand towns; the
weeds will overrun millions of farms if that protection is
taken away."

The speech was unfortunate in its effect upon the Republican party four years later when the Democrats made
extensive use of the dire prophecy, often taken out of its
context, to make it seem that its fulfillment was contingent
on Hoover's defeat. In the interval between the 1932 and

1936 Presidential elections, under the administration of President Franklin D. Roosevelt there had been a marked recovery from the depression. During the Democratic national convention in Philadelphia in 1936, when Roosevelt was nominated for re-election, huge harvester machines were paraded through the streets of Philadelphia bearing placards announcing that they were to be used to mow "Hoover grass."

Hoover was not the first orator to utter the dismal prophecy of grass-grown city streets. William Jennings Bryan in his famous "Cross of Gold" speech at the Democratic national convention in 1896 said: "Burn down your cities and leave our farms, and your cities will spring up again as if by magic; but destroy our farms and the grass will grow in the streets of every city in the country."

Even before Bryan, however, publicists in the South at the outbreak of the war between the States had used this symbol of economic decadence. Edward A. Pollard, editor of the *Daily Richmond Examiner,* in the issue of May 15, 1861, writing of the North's dependence for its prosperity upon the raw materials and trade of the South, predicted that the loss of these bases of wealth consequent upon the war would mean the economic collapse of the United States, and that grass would be growing in the streets of its principal cities. How quickly this prediction was fulfilled was attested by the *Louisville Courier,* which in July 1861, told of grass actually growing in the streets of New York.

"The only thing we have to fear is fear itself."
                                    Franklin Delano Roosevelt

PERHAPS NO President save Lincoln ever had taken office
at so dark an hour in the nation's history as did Franklin
D. Roosevelt on March 4, 1933. The country was in the
throes of the Great Depression, the worst in its history,
which, despite all efforts to cure or alleviate it, grew ever
worse. Europe's business and financial situation was little,
if any, better than our own; Great Britain had gone off the
gold standard and the repercussions of her action were
being felt here.

To climax the country's woeful condition and add to
the gloom and apprehension of all elements of the American people, a sudden bank panic developed in the Middle
West less than a month before the new administration was
due to begin. There were runs on banks by frightened
depositors and several States declared bank holidays in an
effort to prevent the entire system from collapsing.

Nothing that the Hoover administration said or did
was effective to restore public confidence or allay the general fear.

In this fearsome atmosphere the President-elect prepared to take office. Whatever his inward thoughts and
feelings, outwardly he preserved the calm, even buoyant,
demeanor which had become familiar to the American
people. If he shared the general fear, he gave no public
evidence of it. In his determined fight against a crippling
physical malady that had attacked him in his prime he
had shown courage of the highest order and it is obvious
that the condition that confronted him at the very outset
of his term in office did not daunt him. He had declined
to cancel the inaugural parade that for many years had
marked the incoming of a new President and he seemed
determined not to make any concession outwardly to the
prevailing spirit of gloom.

"Nothing is terrible except fear itself", Francis Bacon wrote long ago. It was a sentiment to which Roosevelt could give whole-hearted assent, and in his inaugural address he echoed Bacon's thought in the striking phrase: "The only thing we have to fear is fear itself."

* * *

"A stab in the back."

Franklin Delano Roosevelt

OFTEN IN the case of some striking utterance by a public character his exact words are paraphrased or altered, without in any way changing their meaning, and the altered version is popularly accepted as a verbatim quotation. This is the case with President Franklin D. Roosevelt's indignant denunciation of the action of the Italian government in declaring war on France when that country had been conquered and rendered helpless in the summer of 1940 by Germany. Up to that time Italy had maintained a state of "non-belligerent" neutrality.

"On this tenth day of June 1940," the President declared when Italy's declaration was made known, "the hand that held the dagger has struck it into the back of its neighbor."

This was an unequivocal statement, and the man in the street, understanding it as such, quickly shortened it to the proverbial "stab in the back."

"A new deal for the American people."

Franklin Delano Roosevelt

EVEN BEFORE his election in 1932, Franklin D. Roosevelt, then Governor of New York, indicated the reform character his administration would adopt. He was nominated by the Democratic national convention held in Chicago late in June, and the convention was held over one day in order to enable him to fly from Albany to deliver his speech of acceptance before the whole body of delegates. In his address, the nominee, ringing the changes on President Theodore Roosevelt's "Square Deal," and President Wilson's "New Freedom", proclaimed the "New Deal" in the following passage:

"I pledge you, I pledge myself, to a new deal for the American people. Let us all here assembled constitute ouselves prophets of a new order of competence and courage. This is more than a political campaign; it is a call to arms."

This program, so generally stated, was swiftly formulated and put into action. Within the space of one hundred days the Congress had enacted the major items of the New Deal legislation recommended by the President. These included the Bank Reorganization Act, the National Industrial Recovery Act, an act providing for the reduction of government expenditures by twenty-five percent, the Agricultural Adjustment Act, the Public Works Act providing for the formation of the Civilian Conservation Corps and relief grants to States, and the act establishing the Securities Exchange Commission by which stock exchanges were placed under the jurisdiction of the commission to correct unfair practices in the securities markets.

"The good neighbor."

Franklin Delano Roosevelt

WOODROW WILSON as President laid the foundation of an American policy of amicable relations with the nations of the world by renouncing imperialism and declaring for co-operation with peaceful nations in a stand against violations of treaties and acts of aggression. The Stimson Doctrine, formulated by Secretary of State Henry L. Stimson in the cabinet of President Hoover, was an affirmation of the Wilson policy toward aggressor powers. Under this doctrine the United States, in 1932, refused to recognize the puppet state of Manchukuo which Japan had set up after the seizure of the Chinese territory of Manchuria. As a gesture of neighborliness, Hoover after his election to the presidency in 1928 and just prior to his assuming the office had made a good will voyage to South America. As President in 1930 he began the evacuation of American troops from occupied Latin-American republics and abandoned the asserted right to police countries of Central and South America which might be considered to have been guilty of "wrong-doing."

President Franklin D. Roosevelt in his first inaugural speech on March 4, 1933 declared: "In the field of world policy I would dedicate this nation to the policy of the good neighbor."

In pursuance of this policy he completed during the first year of his term the evacuation of Latin-American republics, affirmed the Stimson Doctrine, and at the Pan-American Conference held in Montevideo late in 1933 accepted a treaty with all American republics, one article of which declared that no state has the right to intervene in the internal or external affairs of another.

"The Nine Old Men."

Drew Pearson (1897-   ) and
Robert Sharon Allen (1900-   )

CRITICISM OF the Supreme Court of the United States by New Deal adherents found concrete presidential support early in the second term of Franklin Delano Roosevelt. Disaffection with the justices of the court was mainly on the ground that because of their mature ages they were ultra-conservative, if not reactionary, in their thinking and in their interpretations of the law, were out of sympathy with the advanced liberal trends of the times and, in general, that the Supreme Court was badly in need of an infusion of new and younger blood.

These views seemed to have been epitomized in the contemptuous characterization, "The Nine Old Men," which was the title of a book by Drew Pearson and Robert S. Allen, Washington news columnists, which was published in 1936.

President Roosevelt himself was believed to share, in some degree at least, the critical opinions concerning the court, and had expressed himself in terms of disappointment at the Court's decision which had resulted in the dissolution of the National Recovery Administration in 1935.

On February 5, 1937, the President sent a message to the Congress recommending the enactment of a measure providing for the appointment of a new judge for each one in the Federal judiciary who had not retired at the age of seventy years after serving at least ten years. This of course included the justices of the Supreme Court whose number, under the law, could be increased to a maximum of fifteen members.

A bill prepared by the Attorney General incorporating the President's recommendations was introduced in the Senate on the same day. In its final form it provided for the retirement of Supreme Court justices on full pay on reaching the age of 75 years, and for the appointment of a co-adjutor justice for any justice not electing to retire at the prescribed age. These coadjutors were invested by the terms of the bill with the same authority and voting power possessed by the justices of the regularly constituted court, and not more than six of them could be appointed by the President, whose appointing power was further limited to one such coadjutor a year.

"The nine old men" comprising the court at the time the bill was introduced were: Chief Justice Charles Evans Hughes, and Associate Justices Oliver Wendell Holmes, Harlan Fiske Stone, Louis D. Brandeis, George Sutherland, Owen J. Roberts, Benjamin Nathan Cardozo, James Clark McReynolds and Pierce Butler.

The President's proposal for the re-formation of the court aroused widespread opposition throughout the nation and in the Congress, and the bill was finally shelved by a vote in the Senate to recommit.

"Straight from the Horse's Mouth."

Joseph Clark Grew (1880-   )

IT REMAINED for a distinguished American statesman to respectabilize and give a place in diplomatic annals to a phrase originating in gamblers' circles. The term "Straight from the horse's mouth," long had been understood among followers of horse racing to mean that a tip on the result of a race came from a source close to the ownership or care of the horse named to win and could be relied on as "a sure thing." In time the phrase gained general currency, to indicate a guaranty of the authoritative nature of some statement or information.

It was so used by Joseph C. Grew, United States Ambassador to Japan, in an address delivered in Tokyo on October 19, 1939, a period when the ever worsening relations between this country and Japan were showing no improvement. The Ambassador had only recently returned to Japan from a five months' leave of absence in the United States during which he had had ample opportunity to acquaint himself with the public, as well as the official, temper toward the Japanese government and people.

During his long stay in Japan as American Ambassador from 1932 to 1942, he had acquired competent knowledge of conditions in Japan, the national psychology, as well as the inner workings of its government. He had observed the growing ascendancy of the military party, the trend towards a totalitarian and fascist government and a clearly developing intent to establish absolute mastery over all Asia. The seizure of Manchuria and the setting up of the puppet state of Manchukuo which our government refused to recognize; the ensuing "China incident," with its ruthless war of rapine, pillage, and spoilation; Japan's formal alliance with fascist powers in the Rome-Berlin-Tokyo axis; and the almost unconcealed hostility of officials and press towards the United States, all evidenced Japan's determination to persist in its course even at the risk of war with this country. The reaction of the United States Government and people, as observed by Mr. Grew, was plainly one of resentment of Japan's course.

Before returning from his leave of absence, the Ambassador had been urged by a Japanese friend here to speak to the people of Japan on the relations between the two countries. While not in agreement with his Japanese friend as to the causes of friction between this country and Japan, Mr. Grew determined that he would discuss the subject frankly on his return to Japan. He did not wish to make his remarks the subject of an official diplomatic paper, and he chose as the occasion for their expression an address before the American-Japan Society. His address was a frank and friendly discussion of the strained relations between his country and Japan, of his observation of American thought during his stay here, and the causes of the rift in the traditional friendship of the two countries.

The opening sentence of the address, "We have a phrase in English, 'straight from the horse's mouth'", was a forthright indication of the plain speaking his audience could expect from him. The address itself, which came to be known as "The Horse's Mouth Speech," while conciliatory in tone, and avowedly made in the interest of better relations between the United States and Japan, left the audience in no doubt as to the actual feelings of the American people and their government toward the government of Japan.

"I shall say it again and again. Your boys are not going to be sent into any foreign wars."

Franklin Delano Roosevelt

FRANKLIN D. ROOSEVELT was re-elected in 1940 upon the issue of keeping this country out of the war then raging overseas. As the campaign cry, "He kept us out of war," had been a winning slogan for Wilson in 1916, the promise of peace for this country proved equally effective twenty-fours years later.

Between the two candidates, Roosevelt, running for a third term, and Wendell L. Willkie, his Republican opponent, there was almost no difference in the foreign policy they advocated for the United States. Both were for keeping this country from being drawn into the World War.

France had only recently been conquered, Italy had abandoned her neutrality to enter the war as an ally of Germany, the Nazi blitzkrieg was devastating England's great cities, and Germany, with Russia her ally and safe from attack on the eastern front, saw victory within her grasp. While the sympathy of a great majority of the American people was with the British, a very considerable element of the population of this country was strongly averse to participation in the war. This so-called isolationist segment looked to the President to maintain the country's neutrality.

In his speech of October 30, 1940, in Boston, Roosevelt pledged American parents to the non-participation of this country in the war in these words: "And while I am talking to you mothers and fathers, I give you one more assurance. I have said this before, but I shall say it again and again and again. Your boys are not going to be sent into any foreign wars."

The President's familiar refrain, "again and again and again," was reminiscent of the limerick quoted by Osbert Sitwell as a favorite of John Sargent, the painter:

> *There was a young lady of Spain*
> *Who often got sick on a train,*
> *Not once and again,*
> *But again and again*
> *And again and again and again.*

* * *

"The Four Freedoms."

Franklin Delano Roosevelt

IN HIS annual message of January 6, 1941 to the Congress in which President Roosevelt asked for the passage of the Lend-Lease measure, he named the four freedoms to which the world must aspire.

"In the future days, which we seek to make secure," the message read, "we look forward to a world founded upon four essential human freedoms."

These, he declared, were: freedom of speech and expression, freedom of worship, freedom from fear, freedom from want.

The first two named by the President are guaranteed in the first of ten amendments to the Constitution and known as the Bill of Rights.

"One World."

Wendell Lewis Willkie (1892-1944)

IN THE presidential campaign of 1940 the Democratic candidate, President Franklin D. Roosevelt and his Republican opponent, Wendell L. Willkie, were generally in agreement as to this country's policies as they affected World War II. Willkie, a veteran of the First World War, was an outstanding leader of the element in his party that opposed isolationism, and after his defeat by Roosevelt his attitude remained unchanged.

The entrance of this country into the war after Pearl Harbor served to increase his interest in the part the United States should take in world affairs when peace should ensue. In order to see for himself what he could of the world, its peoples, leaders, and the battle fronts, he set out on a journey in a Liberator bomber plane, the *Gulliver,* made available to him by President Roosevelt. Forty-nine days were required for his travels of 31,000 miles, in the course of which he visited the Middle East, Turkey, Russia, China, and Siberia, interviewing military leaders, diplomats, merchants, artisans, the man in the street, and government officials. Among the latter were Joseph Stalin, of Russia, and Generalissimo Chiang Kaishek, of China.

The conclusions formed by him as a result of his journeyings were summed up in his book, *One World,* written upon his return. What he observed on his trip impressed upon him the essential unity of the interests of the world and its peoples, necessitating that peace must be planned on this basis, since otherwise there could be no peace for any one part of the world.

"That Man in the White House."

(1935)

BEFORE FRANKLIN D. ROOSEVELT had ended his first term in the Presidency the rift in the relations between him and those elements in business that he characterized as "economic royalists" had widened until it assumed almost the dimensions of a feud. Scornful epithets applied by the President to those who opposed the program of the New Deal were matched by the bitter retorts of his opponents. The most incoherent and least articulate among the latter epitomized their disapproval of the President in the contemptuous expression, "That man in the White House," and the phrase was used variously in private comments by the President's foes and friends.

Among the latter, Frank Kingdon used it for the title of a book which was a defense of the President and a laudation of his administration of his office during three terms as President. Kingdon listed more than a score of the accusations leveled against the President by his critics, and categorically defended him against them.

Principal among the charges against "That man in the White House," which his apologist essayed to refute, were these: that he was a dictator, a communist, a fascist, a revolutionary, a destroyer of capitalism and free enterprise, a coddler of labor, a foe of the Supreme Court, too much a politician, extravagant, and insincere. Furthermore, his critics asserted, and Kingdon denied, the President's New Deal neglected the farmers, he was swinging to the left, to the right, he desired to be President of the United States for life, to establish a family dynasty, to make himself president of the world, that he was destroying the Democratic party and playing up minorities.

"We must constitute ourselves a loyal opposition party."

Wendell Lewis Willkie

THAT IT is the right of a free people both to speak and act, always within the bounds of law, against the policies and acts of government has long been recognized as a prime tenet of democracy's creed. In the Parliament of Great Britain "His (or Her) Majesty's loyal opposition" has been honored as a legitimate unit ever since the responsibility of the sovereign's ministers has been fixed in the British constitution.

The function of an opposition was happily expressed in the phrase uttered by Wendell L. Willkie in his radio address on November 11, 1940, after his unsuccessful campaign for election to the Presidency. In this contest he had polled some 22,000,000 votes against the more than 27,000,000 votes cast for the Democratic incumbent, Franklin D. Roosevelt. The numbers and the ardor of his supporters seemed to Willkie to merit some message to them after his defeat.

"A vital element in the balanced operation of a democracy is a strong, alert and watchful opposition," he told them in his radio address. "That is our task for the next four years. We must constitute ourselves a vigorous, loyal and public-spirited opposition party."

Appealing to his followers to eschew any campaign bitterness and to support the President in building a strong national defense, he said that he himself felt no bitterness, for "We have elected Franklin Roosevelt President. He is your President. He is my President."

In repeating to his supporters that their function was that of "the loyal opposition," he outlined the points of opposition as: the unlimited spending of borrowed money, the growth of bureaucracy, control of elections by political machines, usurpation of powers reserved to the Congress, the subjugation of the courts, concentration of enormous authority in the Executive, discouragement of enterprise, continuance of economic dependence for millions of citizens on government, and verbal provocations of war.

* * *

"The first twelve years are the hardest."

Franklin Delano Roosevelt

ON THE eve of his inauguration as President to a fourth term, President Roosevelt held his regular press conference in the White House, January 19, 1945. The session was given over largely to an exchange of good-humored badinage between the President and the newspaper correspondents.

One of the latter asked the President if he had any reflections on what had been accomplished during the four years of his third term just completed, "and where do we go from here?"

The President's answer was that "The first twelve years are the hardest," using an old expression with an alteration of the number of years. And he added smilingly that the reporters would all give their own interpretation to his answer, and that they "would all guess wrong."

"Clear everything with Sidney."

(*1944*)

ORGANIZED LABOR made its power felt in the presidential campaign of 1944. Both before and after the national conventions were held the Political Action Committee of the Congress of Industrial Organizations was active throughout the country in raising campaign funds, passing on the merits of candidates of both parties for public office, and working for the success of those candidates indorsed by CIO.

In general, the strength of this organization was thrown to the Democratic party and by the time the national convention of that party was held Sidney Hillman, the moving spirit in PAC, had become a powerful voice in the counsels of the Democratic party.

In the convention the only contest was over the choice of the nominee for the Vice Presidency. Henry A. Wallace, the incumbent, was favored for re-election by the New Deal element of the party and also he had the strong indorsement and support of organized labor generally. As objection to Wallace by the conservative wing in the convention grew, it became evident that he could not be nominated and that some other man acceptable to both factions must be chosen.

While the convention was yet in session and seeking to agree on a compromise nominee for Vice President, President Roosevelt stopped briefly in Chicago on his way to the Pacific Coast. He was met by Robert Hannegan, chairman of the Democratic National Committee, who gave him an account of the situation in the convention. In the course of their conference, it was reported, the President told Hannegan to "clear everything with Sidney," meaning thereby that the choice for the Vice Presidential nomination must be agreeable to Hillman.

The phrase, while not admitted by the President or his advisers, was used extensively by the Republicans in the campaign.

"Expedience and justice frequently are not even on speaking terms."

Arthur Hendrick Vandenberg (1884-   )

ONE OF the decisions arrived at in Yalta, the Crimea, in February 1945, among President Roosevelt, Winston Churchill, Prime Minister of Great Britain, and Joseph Stalin, Secretary-General of the Communist Party and head of the Soviet Union, was the summoning of a World Security Conference in San Francisco on April 25, 1945. The purpose of the assemblage, to be composed of delegates from the United Nations, was the framing of a league for world peace to take the place of the ineffectual League of Nations. As one of the bi-partisan delegates to represent this country, President Roosevelt named Arthur H. Vandenberg, Republican, United States Senator from Michigan.

Senator Vandenberg was prominent in his party as an anti-isolationist and an outspoken advocate of the participation of the United States in an organization to promote and maintain world peace. Some of the decisions arrived at in Yalta, however, did not entirely meet his views. Prominent among these was that concerning the treatment of Poland, after the war. The conferees had agreed upon the cession to Russia of Polish territory, the formation of a coalition government and the setting up of a Three-Power Commission in Moscow to treat with a provisional government of Poland.

In a speech in the Senate on March 8, 1945, Senator Vandenberg deplored the "expedient" nature of the plan agreed upon for the treatment of Poland, declaring that all decisions "made under pressure of war" should be "temporary in fact as well as in name." Of the decisions he said: "Inevitably many of them consult expediency. Expediency and justice frequently are not even on speaking terms."

PART TWO

WAR

"One if by land, and two if by sea."

Henry Wadsworth Longfellow (1807-1882)

JOHN HANCOCK and Samuel Adams, New England's fire-brands of the Revolution, were in hiding from the British on the night of April 18, 1775, in the home of a friend in Lexington, twelve miles northwest of Boston. Patriots in that city learned of the intention to send troops to capture them and also to seize ammunition and military supplies stored by the Colonials in Concord.

Paul Revere, a citizen of Boston and an ardent friend of the Colonial cause, arranged to ride to Lexington to warn Hancock and Adams, and thence to Concord, in the event that any movement of troops from Boston was discovered. Booted and spurred for the dash through the countryside, Revere awaited the agreed upon signal:

> . . . . *If the British march*
> *By land or sea from the town tonight,*
> *Hang a lantern aloft in the belfry arch*
> *Of the North Church tower as a signal light,—*
> *One if by land, and two if by sea.*

At midnight he saw two lanterns displayed in the tower of North Church, and forthwith he set out on the ride described in Longfellow's famous verses. He reached Lexington in time to warn Hancock and Adams, on the way arousing the minute men, but he himself was detained at Lexington by British scout troops. A companion, however, rode on to Concord and gave warning. There was a skirmish at Lexington between British troops and the Minute Men, in which the first blood of the Revolution was shed, but the troops were not prevented from going on to Concord.

"The shot heard round the world."

Ralph Waldo Emerson (1803-1882)

"EMBATTLED FARMERS" pitted against trained British troops four times their number launched the greatest revolution in history. There had been ominous rumblings of discontent in the Colonies against the oppressions of the mother country, but there had been no armed insurrection nor was the sentiment for complete independence overwhelming. British troops were quartered in rebellious Boston, however, and the patriots had gathered large quantities of ammunition and military stores in Concord.

When a force of eight hundred British troops from Boston, under command of Lieutenant Colonel Smith and Major Pitcairn, arrived in Concord on the morning of April 19, 1775, to seize the stores, they found a force of two hundred minute men drawn up at the bridge over the Concord river to oppose their passage. The Minute Men refused to disperse at the insolent command of the British officers, a battle ensued and the British were forced to fall back toward Boston. Their retreat was harassed all the way to Lexington by successive ambuscades of the Colonial militia from the aroused countryside. At Lexington they were reinforced by a strong detachment under command of Lord Percy, but the pursuit continued, the Colonists firing with deadly effect from places of concealment. When the harassed redcoats finally reached Charlestown they had suffered the loss of about three hundred of their men.

The heroic resistance of the Massachusetts irregulars greatly heartened American patriots throughout the Colonies. Ralph Waldo Emerson sixty-one years later wrote the beautiful four-stanza *Concord Hymn* which was sung at the dedication of the battle monument on April 19, 1836. The first stanza is:

> By the rude bridge that arched the flood,
> Their flag to April's breeze unfurled,
> Here once the embattled farmers stood,
> And fired the shot heard 'round the world.

* * *

"In the name of the great Jehovah and the Continental Congress."

Ethan Allen (1738-1789)

In this resounding phrase Ethan Allen leading the "Green Mountain Boys" demanded the surrender of Fort Ticonderoga at the head of Lake Champlain. Some historians contend that Allen's demand was couched in terms much more profane and less heroic than those of the popularly accepted legend.

At any rate the surprised British officer in command of the fort surrendered it early in the morning of May 10, 1775.

Allen was taken prisoner by the British in September of the same year and held until exchanged in May 1778.

"Don't fire until you see the whites of their eyes."

William Prescott (1726-1795)

FIFTEEN HUNDRED American troops under the command of Colonel William Prescott obeyed his order with such deadly effect at the Battle of Bunker Hill, June 17, 1775, that the charge of a superior British force was bloodily repulsed.

It was the first severe engagement of the Revolution, fought at a time when the American army had not yet been organized and consisted of raw and undisciplined recruits. As part of a general plan to drive the British troops from Boston, Prescott's force under cover of night had fortified Breed's Hill near Bunker Hill, Charlestown. When the British discovered the earthworks in the morning the position was fired upon by their ships and forts.

A force of 3,000 British troops then was landed and advanced on the American works. Twice their charges were repulsed, but a third attempt was successful, for the powder supply of the Americans was exhausted and they were forced to retreat across Charlestown Neck.

"I only regret that I have but one life to lose for my country."

Nathan Hale (1755-1776)

IN LOSING his life for his country Nathan Hale gained immortality for his name. The sacrifice was made in the performance of a hazardous task undertaken at the request of George Washington, Commander-in-Chief of the Continental Army. He badly needed information about the British forces on Long Island and asked the commander of Knowlton's Rangers, then operating in the vicinity of New York, to obtain it for him.

Hale, who was a captain in the Rangers, volunteered for the attempt and in the disguise of a Dutch schoolmaster he penetrated the British lines on Long Island early in September, 1776. After obtaining the desired information he set about to return to his own command, but was captured by the British when near his own picket lines on September 21.

He freely told his captors his name, rank, and purpose of his entrance within their lines, and he was condemned to die as a spy the next morning. On the gallows the young patriot's last words were:

"I only regret that I have but one life to lose for my country."

Hale was twenty-one years old when he died. He was a native of Connecticut and one of nine brothers, six of whom served in the Revolution. He had entered the Continental Army as a lieutenant on January 1, 1776, and soon afterwards was promoted to a captaincy.

"Or Molly Stark is a widow tonight."

John Stark (1728-1822)

GENERAL BURGOYNE'S expedition from Canada into New York in the summer of 1777, met its first serious check at the Battle of Bennington on August 16. It was the first of a series of defeats which culminated in the surrender of Burgoyne's British troops at Saratoga in October. Burgoyne had taken Ticonderoga on July 6, and dispatched a force of 500 troops and a horde of Indians led by Colonel Baum to seize military stores at Bennington, Vermont. There on the outskirts of the town a force of 1400 New Hampshire militia and Green Mountain Boys commanded by John Stark of New Hampshire confronted the British troops.

Stark's signal for the attack was given in the words: "There, my boys, are your enemies, redcoats and tories. You must beat them—or Molly Stark is a widow tonight."

The Americans beat them decisively, almost annihilating Baum's troops. When reinforcements of 600 Hessians under Colonel Breyman came up later, the Americans defeated them also. In this battle the British lost more than 900 effectives, the Americans, 82. Stark received the thanks of the Congress and was made a brigadier-general in the Continental Army.

One version of Stark's actual words in referring to his wife is: "Or my wife sleeps a widow tonight." As her given name was Elizabeth, it is puzzling to account for the generally accepted quotation in which she is called "Molly."

"These are the times that try men's souls."

Thomas Paine (1737-1809)

AFTER A series of crushing defeats, including those of the battles of Long Island, Harlem Heights and White Plains and the capture of Fort Washington and Fort Lee, Washington's depleted army was in retreat across New Jersey in the Fall of 1776. Thomas Paine, an English immigrant who earlier in the year had written *Common Sense,* in which he argued for complete independence for the Colonies, joined the beaten troops as they fled towards Philadelphia. Untrained, undisciplined, ragged, and ill-fed, Washington's army was demoralized, miserable, and disintegrating as desertions increased. There was a general lack of confidence on the part of the men in their leaders or the success of the Revolution, whose fortunes seemed to be at their lowest ebb.

Paine had shared the hardships of the weary marchers, listened to the despairing talk of the men in the ranks and he sensed that the situation was desperate. At the suggestion of some of the officers, including, it is said, Washington himself, he decided to write an appeal to the patriotism of the troops in an effort to restore their morale. With a drumhead for a desk and by the light of a bivouac fire, he wrote *The American Crisis,* whose opening sentences are:

"These are the times that try men's souls. The summer soldier and the sunshine patriot will, in this crisis, shrink from the services of their country; but he that stands it now, deserves the love and thanks of man and woman. . . ."

The appeal was first printed in the *Pennsylvania Journal* of December 1776. Afterwards it was reprinted in pamphlet form as *The American Crisis, No. 1.*

"I've just begun to fight."

> John Paul Jones (*1747-1792*)

BORN A SCOT, John Paul Jones had come to America, taken up the cause of the colonists against the mother country, and late in 1775 was commissioned a lieutenant in the Continental Navy then forming. He was put in command of the *Alfred* which he had outfitted and which was the first American naval vessel to fly the Continental flag.

Jones soon acquired a reputation as a privateer because of his depredations and captures of enemy shipping, and in 1778 he was put in command of the *Ranger,* with which he raided the Scottish coast. In August 1779, in command of the *Bonhomme Richard,* named in compliment to Benjamin Franklin, he led a little fleet of five naval vessels and two privateers, sailing from France for West Ireland. Thence his flotilla rounded the Scottish coast to the east coast of Yorkshire, England.

Off Flamborough Head, on September 23, 1779, Jones' fleet fell in with forty-one sail in the Baltic trade convoyed by two British men-of-war, the *Serapis,* Captain Richard Pearson commanding, and the *Countess of Scarborough,* commander Thomas Percy. In the desperate battle that ensued the guns of the *Bonhomme Richard* and the *Serapis* at times were almost muzzle to muzzle. Jones maneuvered the *Richard* alongside the British war ship and succeeded in lashing them together stem to stern. The *Richard,* a twelve-pounder pitted against the *Serapis,* an eighteen-pounder, was so badly damaged and leaking that only her pumps saved her from sinking and both ships were afire several times during the engagement.

When the *Richard's* condition seemed hopeless, Captain Pearson signaled Jones, "Have you struck?" To which Jones replied,

"I've just begun to fight."

The engagement ended only when, after three hours of carnage, the *Serapis* struck its colors.

"There never was a good war or a bad peace."

Benjamin Franklin

BENJAMIN FRANKLIN was one of the commissioners, along with John Adams, John Jay, Thomas Jefferson, and Henry Laurens, appointed to negotiate the treaty of peace with Great Britain at the end of the War of the Revolution. The negotiations were carried on in Paris, and the treaty was signed on September 3, 1783.

The venerable philosopher's well known opinions about war and peace found pithy expression in a letter written September 11, of that year to Josiah Quincy. "May we never see another war!" he wrote. "For in my opinion there never was a good war or a bad peace."

This sentiment he repeated in a letter to Dr. Shipley, Bishop of Asaph, as well as in a letter to Mrs. Mary Hewson, dated January 27, 1783, at Passy, France. To her he wrote: "At length we are at peace. God be praised, and long, very long, may it continue! All wars are follies. Very expensive, and very mischievous ones."

* * *

"Don't give up the ship."

James Lawrence (1781-1813)

THIS WAS the last command given by Commander Lawrence, U.S.N., as he lay dying in the cockpit of his frigate the *Chesapeake* in the afternoon of June 1, 1813.

The *Chesapeake* cruising off Boston well out to sea had met H.M.S. *Shannon,* and the bloodiest sea fight of the War of 1812 ensued. Lawrence was shot through the lungs and carried below. As he heard the tramp of the British boarding party on the deck above him, he raised himself and gave the order:

"Don't give up the ship! Sink her, blow her up!"

The Americans fought desperately, but they were over-powered and the Chesapeake was taken.

"We will greet you with bloody hands and welcome you to hospitable graves."

Thomas Corwin (1794-1865)

THE SEED of war with Mexico was planted when the United States annexed Texas in 1845. The annexation had been vigorously opposed by anti-slavery elements in this country who rightly foresaw by it the extension of slave territory. The Whig party had fought and lost its campaign in 1844 on the issue of opposition to annexation, and when the Congress on May 13, 1845, declared war against Mexico the party's adherents continued unreconciled to the course of President Polk's administration.

Thomas Corwin, Whig Senator from Ohio, was one of the most outspoken of the critics of the war, which he considered unjust and based on a policy of conquest. Corwin, who was popularly called "Tom," was noted for his oratory of a breezy, witty, and vigorous style, and for his quickness of retort in debate. In a speech in the Senate on February 11, 1846, opposing further appropriations for the conduct of the war, he denounced "destiny doctrine" and the war generally. When Lewis Cass interrupted with the statement, which was of the pattern of the usual justification of territorial aggressions, that "we want room," Corwin retorted:

"If I were a Mexican, I would tell you, 'Have you not enough room in your own country to bury your dead men? If you come into mine, we will greet you with bloody hands and welcome you to hospitable graves.' "

This impassioned utterance was regarded by some as little short of treasonable and it had an adverse effect upon Corwin's political fortunes, at least in so far as elective office was concerned. Yet, as James Ford Rhodes, the historian, comments, this passage from Corwin's speech differs little, if any, from the sentiment expressed in the speech of the elder Pitt delivered at the time of the American Revolution. In that speech Pitt declared:

"If I were an American, as I am an Englishman, while a foreign troop was landed in my country I never would lay down my arms—Never—never—never!"

* * *

"We have met the enemy and they are ours."

Oliver Hazard Perry (1785-1819)

WRITTEN IN pencil on the back of an old letter, this was Commodore Perry's announcement of his victory over the British in the naval Battle of Lake Erie on September 10, 1813. On that day, Perry, in command of the American fleet of three brigs, five schooners and one sloop, had met a British fleet of superior strength at Put-in-Bay.

An engagement ensued lasting three and a quarter hours, ending with the surrender of the British fleet. Perry's report to General William Henry Harrison, in command of the Army in the Northwest, was written immediately after the surrender, and to his laconic announcement of the victory he added the toll of captured vessels:

"Two ships, two brigs, one schooner and one sloop."

"Remember the Alamo."

(1836)

WHEN THE Texans revolted against Mexico late in 1835 General Sam Houston was made president of the Lone Star Republic. In February 1836 General Santa Anna with an army of 4,000 Mexicans marched against San Antonio and surrounded the Alamo, a fort built within the city.

After a siege lasting nearly a month the fort was taken by assault and all its one hundred and eighty defenders were massacred, among them Davy Crockett and Colonel James Bowie.

A month later Houston's Texans at San Jacinto defeated the Mexicans under Santa Anna, who was taken prisoner. As the Texans fought the battle which was to win their independence from Mexico their battle cry was "Remember the Alamo!" In his report of the battle, General Houston wrote that the attack was led by the regiment commanded by Colonel Sidney Sherman, whose men advanced in double quick time, "singing the war cry, Remember the Alamo."

"If any man attempts to haul down the American flag, shoot him on the spot."

John Adams Dix (1798-1879)

As PRESIDENT BUCHANAN's administration drew to its close and secession sentiment in the South became more intense, there were threats of the seizure of Federal property in the dissident States. John Adams Dix, Secretary of the Treasury in Buchanan's cabinet, in an official dispatch on January 29, 1861, ordered the Treasury office in New Orleans to take possession of a revenue cutter at that port, adding:

"If any man attempts to haul down the American flag, shoot him on the spot."

Dix was a former United States Senator from New York who had broken with the Democratic party on the slavery question. He held the office of secretary of the treasury only a few months and upon Lincoln's accession to the Presidency he was succeeded by Salmon P. Chase.

"See, there is Jackson, standing like a stone wall."
Bernard Elliott Bee (1823-1861)

IT WAS in the first Battle of Bull Run that the Confederate general, Thomas Jonathan Jackson, got the name which he later made famous. The battle, also known as the Battle of Manassas, was fought on July 21, 1861, near a small creek, Bull Run, in northeastern Virginia, and was the first important engagement between Union and Confederate armies. Some eighteen thousand troops on each side, both armies almost untrained militia, were engaged, the Union forces under General Irwin McDowell, the Confederates under Generals Pierre G. T. Beauregard and Jackson.

The battle began early in the forenoon and continued until nearly three o'clock in the afternoon, by which time victory for the Union forces seemed certain. Throughout the engagement, however, Jackson's brigade, which was stationed on a small hill, remained immovable, repelling stubbornly all charges against it and evoking the admiration of the Confederate Brigadier General Bernard E. Bee, who was killed soon after. Observing the tenacity with which the brigade kept its position, Bee exclaimed: "See, there is Jackson, standing like a stone wall."

Until reinforcements came up for the sorely beset Confederates, Jackson's men held their position. Then the strengthened army drove the Federal troops from the field, turning into a rout what had seemed certain victory for McDowell's troops.

"All Quiet Along the Potomac."

George Brinton McClellan (1826-1885)

AFTER THE first Battle of Bull Run the hopes of the Union were centered upon Major General George B. McClellan. The disastrous rout of Union forces in the first considerable meeting of the opposing forces convinced the North that the conquest of the Confederacy was a task for able generalship. President Lincoln put McClellan in command of the Army of the Potomac and upon the retirement of General Winfield Scott, McClellan was appointed his successor in command of the Armies of the United States.

It was the task of the Army of the Potomac to take Richmond, the capital of the Confederate States. The cry throughout the Union was "On to Richmond!" but between McClellan's army and the Confederate capital were General Lee and his Army of Virginia.

Conceded to be an able commander, McClellan, in his Fabian policy in the conduct of the campaign to take Richmond, stirred the President to insistence upon a forward movement. The stubborn streak in McClellan's nature and the repeated reports from his headquarters, "All quiet along the Potomac," exasperated the public clamorous for action, and McClellan at length was superseded as Commander in Chief by General Halleck.

After the second Bull Run, McClellan was again put in command of the Army of the Potomac, but following the inconclusive Battle of Antietam he was again relieved of his command and thereafter had no part in the conduct of the war.

"We Are Coming, Father Abraham, Three Hundred Thousand More."

James Sloan Gibbons (1810-1892)

Six days after Abraham Lincoln's inauguration as President, Fort Sumter fell under the bombardment of Beauregard's artillery. Forts Moultrie and Pinckney had been seized by the Confederates, a provisional constitution had been adopted and a Confederate government set up in Montgomery, Alabama, and it had issued a call for 20,000 volunteers to fight in the cause of Secession. No longer could any doubt exist that only by war could the Union be preserved.

President Lincoln's first call for volunteers, issued on April 15, 1861, was for 75,000 men, and a blockade of Southern ports was proclaimed. The Confederacy then passed a general conscription law. On May 3, Lincoln called for additional volunteers, and three weeks later United States troops invaded Virginia. The Congress in the meantime had voted 500,000 more men for the armies and half a billion dollars for the prosecution of the war.

To aid the raising of a volunteer Union army, James Sloan Gibbons, a Quaker abolitionist of Delaware, wrote a stirring marching song, the first line of which was: "We are coming, Father Abraham, three hundred thousand more." It first appeared in the New York *Evening Post* on July 16, 1862, and in that same year was set to music by Patrick Sarsfield Gilmore, bandmaster of the Twenty-fourth Massachusetts Regiment.

The authorship of the song at first was attributed to William Cullen Bryant, who disclosed that Gibbons had written it.

"Unconditional and immediate surrender."
Ulysses Simpson Grant (1822-1885)

GENERAL GRANT gained his soubriquet, "Unconditional Surrender," by his stern reply to the proposal for an armistice made by General S. B. Buckner, the Confederate commander defending Fort Donelson, on the left bank of the Cumberland River in Tennessee. Grant had taken the companion Fort Henry, on the right bank of the Tennessee River, twelve miles distant, on February 6, 1862, and six days later moved on Fort Donelson.

On the morning of February 16, when the fort had been under incessant attack for three days, General Buckner asked for an armistice until noon of that day and the appoinment of commissioners to settle terms of capitulation. Grant's reply was:

"No terms except an unconditional and immediate surrender can be accepted. I propose to move immediately upon your works."

Buckner then surrendered the fort with its garrison of more than twelve thousand men, forty guns, and a large supply of ammunition.

"I always make it a rule to get there first with the most men."

Nathan Bedford Forrest (1821-1877)

IT IS unlikely that Lieutenant General Nathan Bedford Forrest, famed Confederate cavalry leader, ever studied Napoleon's career or that the Corsican's military maxims were familiar to him. Yet the phrase by which Forrest is best known to many is one reminiscent of Napoleon's aphorism that God is on the side of the heaviest artillery.

Of keen intelligence but with little formal education, Forrest, from a private in the ranks in 1861, advanced by rapid stages until at the end of the Civil War he was a lieutenant general and conceded to be one of the foremost leaders of the Confederate forces and one of the greatest military men of his time.

Although he had had no prior military training, he was an able strategist, a resourceful tactician and extraordinarily successful in coping with the problems of logistics in a period when the word itself possessed little meaning for the average officer of the line. His handling of his troops did not follow conventional cavalry practices. He had little use for sabers, preferring carbines and pistols, and frequently dismounted his men and had them fight as infantry. His guiding principle of warfare was attack! attack! and in the four years of his service, raiding and fighting incessantly in Kentucky, Tennessee, Georgia, Mississippi, and Alabama, he was the scourge of his Union foes, and his highly mobile operations were a cause of great concern to General Sherman on his march to the sea, as well as to General Grant then waging the decisive campaign in Virginia.

The wording of the phrase generally attributed to Forrest, "Git thar fustest with the mostest," seems to be of dubious authenticity. His biographers are agreed that he was unlettered, but by no means illiterate or of the "cracker" or hill-billy" type of the South. Although his speech was ungrammatical, his spelling phonetic, and his pronunciation that of the rural people among whom he lived, support seems to be lacking for the grotesque phrasing attributed to him.

As quoted by his most recent biographer, Robert Selph Henry, Forrest's exact words, on the authority of Captain Lewis M. Hosea, a member of a Federal party that met Forrest to discuss an exchange of prisoners, were: "I always make it a rule to get there first with the most men."

Whatever Forrest's exact words, they seem to have represented an aspiration rather than a reality, for his fighting was done more often with troops inferior in numbers to those of the enemy. But he had the faculty of so disposing them as to create the illusion of "the most," and he demonstrated frequently that he could "get there first."

* * *

"I propose to fight it out on this line if it takes all summer."

Ulysses Simpson Grant

On March 9, 1864, Grant was made lieutenant general in command of all the armies of the United States in the Civil War. In May began the fight through the Wilderness in the advance on Richmond, capital of the Confederacy. The losses of the Army of the Potomac were very heavy, but Grant doggedly kept his face turned toward Richmond.

His determination to maintain the campaign as he had planned it, despite losses and reverses, was expressed in a dispatch to Washington written on May 11, 1864, before Spottsylvania Court House, where his attack on Lee's forces had been repulsed with great slaughter.

"The cheese box on a raft."

(1862)

A REVOLUTIONARY innovation in naval architecture, which was destined to evolve into the modern turreted warships and which had an important contributory part in deciding the issue of the Civil War, at first excited only ridicule.

The *Monitor,* a squat vessel with a round iron tower for a superstructure on a low deck, was contemptuously referred to as "the cheese box on a raft," and the "tin can on a shingle," when on the morning of March 9, 1862, it steamed out into Hampton Roads to do battle with the Confederate ironclad *Merrimac.*

The *Merrimac* had been rebuilt from the forty-gun steam frigate scuttled by the Federals when they abandoned Norfolk Navy Yard the year before. Renamed the *Virginia* by the Confederates into whose hands it fell, the ironclad was a powerful acquisition by the small Confederate Navy in its efforts to break the Union blockade of Southern ports.

The day before the engagement with the *Monitor,* the *Merrimac* had cruised in the waters off Newport News where several Federal men-of-war lay under the guns of the fort. Regardless of the shells from the fort and the warships, which were ineffective against her armor, the frigate attacked the vessels, grounding the 50-gun *Congress* and capturing the 30-gun *Cumberland* and her crew.

The next day the *Monitor* steamed forth to challenge the victorious frigate in an engagement that was the first action in history between two steam-driven ironclad men-of-war. The *Monitor* had been designed by John Ericsson, Swedish inventor, and was a type not only wholly new but also of unconventional lines and appearance. Its length was 172 feet, beam 41, and it drew only ten feet of water, which was less than half the draft of the *Merrimac.* Her armanent consisted of only two guns mounted in the turret, but they were revolved by machinery and fired 180-pound shot.

In the fight, which lasted four hours, the *Merrimac* was hard pressed by the strange looking craft and made many attempts to ram her, but the *Monitor's* greater maneuverability enabled her to avoid the attacks. Although outnumbered twenty-fold in guns by the *Merrimac,* the *Monitor's* fire power was superior because of its ability to direct its guns effectively from any position and also by reason of the greater weight of its projectiles.

The engagement ended with the *Monitor* unharmed and the Merrimac seriously disabled and forced to withdraw up the Elizabeth river.

Technically, it was a drawn battle, but actually a Federal victory, for it enabled the Union to tighten the blockade of Confederate ports and thus materially contribute to the eventual collapse of the Confederacy.

* * *

"You may fire when you are ready, Gridley."

George Dewey (1837-1917)

WITH THIS signal from Commodore Dewey, Captain Charles Vernon Gridley, commanding the flagship *Olympia,* opened the Battle of Manila Bay on the morning of May 1, 1898. Dewey, in command of the United States Asiatic fleet, and Gridley were warm personal friends, and the honor of beginning the historic engagement was evidence of their friendship.

In a few hours the American naval force had destroyed the entire Spanish fleet of ten vessels and 643 of its officers and men, without the loss of a man or ship of the American fleet.

For this exploit Dewey was immediately made rear admiral, and admiral next year. *The Olympia's* commander, who was in poor health at the time of the battle, survived it by only a few months.

"Damn the torpedoes! Go ahead!"

David Glasgow Farragut (1801-1870)

FARRAGUT, FIRST admiral of the United States Navy, at the attack on the Confederate defenses in Mobile Bay, August 5, 1864, observed the operations of his fleet from the rigging of his flagship the *Hartford*. Mobile's defenders had stretched a double line of torpedoes for a distance of three miles, leaving only a narrow channel for their own blockade runners. The monitor *Tecumseh,* leading the Federal line, struck a torpedo (really a mine) and sank. The *Brooklyn,* just ahead of the flagship, halted and the entire line was held up.

"What is the matter?" Farragut asked.

"Torpedoes," came the answer.

"Damn the torpedoes! Go ahead!" he ordered.

Then Farragut's fleet of twenty-five vessels steamed into the harbor, after silencing Forts Morgan and Gaines at the entrance of Mobile Bay, and destroyed the Confederate fleet of an ironclad ram and four gunboats.

"Hold the fort! I am coming."

William Tecumseh Sherman (1820-1891)

As GENERAL W. T. SHERMAN prepared for his famous march to the sea, General John M. Corse, in command of a division under him held a pass near Allatoona, Georgia. Facing Corse's division of 2000 troops was the Confederate army of General John B. Hood.

It was important to the success of Sherman's plans that the pass be held, and from the top of Kenesaw Mountain on October 5, 1864, General Sherman signaled Corse: "Hold out; relief is coming."

The battle for the pass raged all day. Although his force had been cut down in the bloody fighting to one-third its original strength and he himself was badly wounded, Corse refused to surrender and nightfall saw the pass still held by his soldiers.

On the morning of the second day as Sherman's men marched to Corse's relief, they saw a signal from Allatoona announcing:

"We hold out. Corse here."

Sherman's signaled order to Corse became a popular rallying cry of those loyal to the Union. The change in the exact wording of his message was due to the general acceptance as his of the words "Hold the fort", which were used in a popular gospel hymn.

"War is hell."

William Tecumseh Sherman

PACIFISTS AND realists alike are fond of quoting this famous dictum. While its history is vague, those who knew Sherman agree that it accurately represented his feelings about war. Bartlett's *Quotations,* edited by Christopher Morley and Louella D. Everett, states that a letter published in the *National Tribune,* Washington, D. C., November 26, 1914, attributes the quotation to an address delivered by Sherman before the graduating class of the Michigan Military Academy on June 19, 1879. The part of the address quoted is as follows:

"I am sick and tired of war. Its glory is all moonshine. It is only those who have never fired a shot nor heard the shrieks and groans of the wounded who cry aloud for blood, more vengeance, more desolation. War is hell."

According to the *Dictionary of American Biography,* edited by Dumas Malone, Sherman's expression was, "War . . . is all hell," and was contained in an address Sherman delivered in Columbus, Ohio, on August 11, 1880, which was reported the next day in the *Ohio State Journal.*

"You furnish the pictures and I'll furnish the war."

William Randolph Hearst (1863-   )

NEWSPAPER RIVALRY for circulation reached its highest point in New York City in 1918 when Joseph Pulitzer and William Randolph Hearst contended for public favor for their newspapers. The Pulitzer newspaper properties consisted of the *Morning World* and the *Evening World* in New York and the *Post-Dispatch* in St. Louis, while Hearst's newspapers were published in cities from coast to coast. Competition for circulation was keenest, however, in New York, and both Pulitzer and Hearst utilized the Cuban insurrection and the impending declaration of hostilities between the United States and Spain as a source of sensational news articles to increase the circulations of their newspapers.

Following the sinking of the United States battleship *Maine* in Havana harbor on February 15, 1898, and in anticipation of this country's formal declaration of war against Spain, Hearst sent Frederic Remington, the painter, to Cuba in March to provide material to illustrate the dispatches from Cuba published in his newspapers. Remington could find no war scenes to paint, however, and so reported to Hearst, who replied: "Please remain. You furnish the pictures and I'll furnish the war."

The United States declared war on April 22, 1898, and by many who opposed it Hearst was blamed for having had a large share in bringing it about. Although privately he denied ever having sent the message to Remington, he never publicly disavowed it.

"Remember the Maine."

(1898)

WAR BETWEEN the United States and Spain became inevitable when the United States battleship *Maine* was mysteriously destroyed by an explosion while at anchor in the harbor of Havana on February 15, 1898. The American people generally were convinced that the sinking of the warship was the result of an act of treachery by the officials of a government with which we were at peace, although this has never been established as proved fact. Public passions were aroused and "Remember the Maine" became a war cry, as "Remember the Alamo" had been years before.

A little less than two months after the sinking of the Maine this country declared war on Spain. The nation was ripe for it, because its sympathies were with Cuba which for years had been governed by a succession of Spanish Captains-General whose tyrannical rule caused recurrent uprising, culminating in a stubborn revolt led by General Garcia. The harsh measures of the Captain-General, Weyler, known as "Butcher" Weyler, against the insurgents caused indignation throughout this country and an active war party had demanded American intervention in behalf of the Cubans.

The resultant Spanish-American War was ended by the Treaty of December 10, 1898, and Cuba became an independent nation.

"Carry a message to Garcia."

Elbert Hubbard (1850-1915)

HUBBARD'S ARTICLE, in which this famous line appeared, was published in his magazine *The Philistine* of March 1900. The article, in Hubbard's usual homiletic vein, was occasioned by a hazardous voyage made by a young American Army officer in April 1898, just after this country had declared war on Spain.

In line with the Army's policy to give all aid to the Cuban revolutionists, Lieutenant Andrew Summers Rowan, of the Army Intelligence service, was sent to get in touch with the Cuban insurgent leader, General Calixto Garcia, somewhere in Cuba. Rowan's mission was attended by many dangers, but he succeeded in landing in an open boat on Cuban soil near Turquino Peak on April 24, 1898. Having sought out and found Garcia, he returned to Washington with the desired information about the insurgent army.

The sentence in Hubbard's article containing the much quoted line follows:

"It is not book learning young men need, nor instruction about this and that, but a stiffening of the vertebrae which will cause them to be loyal to a trust, to act promptly, concentrate their energies, do a thing—'carry a message to Garcia.' "

"Don't cheer, men; the poor fellows are dying."
John Woodward Philip (1840-1900)

CAPTAIN "JACK" PHILIP was in command of the battleship *Texas* when Admiral Cervera's fleet of Spanish warships steamed out of Santiago harbor to meet the blockading American warships of Commodore William T. Sampson's Atlantic Squadron on July 3, 1898. When the Battle of Santiago ended a few hours later Cervera's entire fleet of four armored cruisers and three torpedo destroyers had been sunk under the fire of the American fleet.

At one period in the battle the fire of the entire American fleet was concentrated on the *Viscaya*, Cervera's flagship, and soon the cruiser was in flames. An explosion followed which doomed the vessel and as the Spanish colors fell the men aboard the *Texas* began to cheer.

Captain Philip, looking out upon the destruction of the Spanish fleet and the waters filled with the dead and wounded and struggling survivors, said:

"Don't cheer, men; the poor fellows are dying."

More than five hundred officers and men of Cervera's fleet were killed, wounded, or drowned and 1700 taken prisoners. Not an American vessel was lost or badly damaged, and only one man was killed and one seriously wounded.

"The sun will go down on a million men in arms."

William Jennings Bryan

As THIS country in the second year of President Wilson's administration began slowly drifting toward participation in the World War, Secretary of State Bryan was greatly disquieted by the growing sentiment in the nation for some sort of military preparedness. Among both the supporters and opponents of the administration there were advocates for the adoption of measures that would put the nation in a state of readiness for any eventuality. Germany had not yet declared its unrestricted submarine warfare, but the temper of the Imperial Government was well known and it was generally realized by Americans that the depredations of German naval vessels might well involve this nation in war.

The discussion of preparedness, including provision of universal military training, moved Bryan to issue a public statement, the most striking part of which was: "The President knows that if this country needed a million men, and needed them in a day, the call would go out at sunrise and the sun would go down on a million men in arms."

This optimistic opinion was widely derided as a failure by Mr. Bryan to recognize the realities of the situation.

"There's glory enough for all."

Winfield Scott Schley (1839-1909)

THE GREAT naval battle of Santiago, in which a Spanish fleet was destroyed by American men-of-war on July 3, 1898, and Spain lost Cuba and Porto Rico, her sole remaining possessions in the Western Hemisphere, gave rise to a bitter controversy. In essence, the dispute was as to which one of the two high-ranking American naval officers participating in the sea fight should rightfully have the credit for the victory.

The Spanish fleet of Admiral Pascual Cervera was bottled up in the harbor of Santiago de Cuba, where in late June it had taken refuge from the blockading American warships of Commodore William T. Sampson's North Atlantic Squadron and Commodore Winfield S. Schley's Flying Squadron. The American blockaders stood on guard outside the harbor while the forces of Major General William R. Shafter, commanding the American volunteer army, fought to a favorable decision the battle of San Juan and El Caney.

At nine o'clock in the morning of July 3, Sampson, who was senior in command of the blockading fleet, proceeded eastward aboard his flagship the *New York* for a conference with General Shafter seven miles distant. Thirty-five minutes later Cervera's warships steamed out of Santiago harbor and proceeded westward in an attempt to escape. Schley, commanding in the absence of Sampson, ordered pursuit and a general engagement followed, ending at 1:15 in the afternoon when the last of the six cruisers and three destroyers was put out of action and Cervera and other Spanish officers were taken prisoners. Sampson's flagship, which at no time had been out of sight of the action, reached the column at two o'clock.

The city of Santiago was formally surrendered to Shafter on July 17, by the Spanish General Toral, virtually ending the war. The elation of the American people, however was marred somewhat by the bitter dispute, which raged in the Navy personnel as well as in the press and in the Congress, as to whether Sampson or Schley was responsible for the victory. It was generally conceded that the battle plan was Sampson's, but Schley, in directing the actual fighting assumed that he was in chief command in the absence of Sampson from the scene. His comment on the controversy was, that in view of the completeness of the victory, "There's glory enough for all."

Both Sampson and Schley were advanced to the rank of rear admiral in recognition of their services.

* * *

"Too proud to fight."

[*Thomas*] *Woodrow Wilson*

AT A time when American sympathy was divided as between the Central Europe powers and the Allied nations in World War I, President Wilson addressed an assemblage of foreign-born citizens in Philadelphia on May 10, 1915. In that speech he declared that, "There is such a thing as a man being too proud to fight." The phrase caused widespread criticism, especially among those who favored the cause of the Allies, and it was condemned as a pusilanimous expression of extreme pacifism.

Wilson himself believed that the phrase was misinterpreted, and his apologists contended that misinterpretation was due to the separation of a single sentence from its immediate context. Fairly construed, they maintained, the President's words meant that there was available a reliance other than a resort to war for the settlement of differences with Germany. Furthermore, it was explained, the phrase sought to inculcate the virtue of self-mastery, which at times could be more heroic than fighting.

"A fight or a frolic."

Robley Dunglison Evans (1846-1912)

RELATIONS BETWEEN the United States and Japan became acutely strained in 1906 over the action of the San Francisco school board refusing to admit Japanese, Chinese and Korean children to the regular public schools and directing that they attend special schools provided for them. The Japanese government protested that the treaty of 1894 accorded to their nationals resident in the United States the status of citizens of "the most favored nation," and that hence the order of the San Francisco school board was a violation of their rights. The comments of newspapers in both California and Japan served to aggravate the controversy, which was only settled by the "Gentlemen's Agreement" of 1907, whereby California permitted the attendance of Japanese children under sixteen years of age at the regular public schools, and the Japanese government promised to stop the emigration of Japanese labor to this country.

As a demonstration of the naval strength of this country, and furthermore as notice to Japan that the settlement of the California exclusion question was not because of any fear of Japan, President Theodore Roosevelt late in the year decided to send a fleet of American war vessels on a cruise around the world. Accordingly a fleet of twenty-eight men-of-war left Hampton Roads, Virginia, on December 16, 1907, on the start of the cruise. The fleet was in command of Rear Admiral Robley D. Evans, who as a captain had commanded the battleship *Iowa* in the Battle of Santiago during the Spanish-American War of 1898. Evans, who was popularly known as "Fighting Bob," prior to the sailing of the fleet, commented that it was ready for "A fight or a frolic."

In his autobiography, published several years after the cruise, Roosevelt in reviewing this event in his administration, referred to the personnel of the men-of-war as, in Evans' phrase, "game for a fight or a frolic."

While the cruise, as it eventuated, was not exactly a "frolic," there was no fighting, for the fleet was received with honors at the Japanese ports it visited.

* * *

"Lafayette, we are here."

Charles E. Stanton (1859-1933)

CONTRARY TO widespread belief, this was not the utterance of General Pershing, but of an American Army officer whom he had delegated to speak in his stead. The famous phrase was the closing sentence of a short speech made by Colonel Charles E. Stanton, chief disbursing officer of the A.E.F., at the tomb of Lafayette in Picpus Cemetery, Paris, on July 4, 1917.

Colonel Stanton, a nephew of Lincoln's famous secretary of war, Edwin M. Stanton, in his address at Lafayette's tomb said:

"America has joined forces with the Allied Powers, and what we have of blood and treasure are yours. Therefore it is that with loving pride we drape the colors in tribute of respect to this citizen of your great republic. And here and now in the presence of the illustrious dead we pledge our hearts and our honor in carrying this war to a successful issue. Lafayette, we are here."

"A strict accountability."

[Thomas] Woodrow Wilson

UNRESTRICTED SUBMARINE warfare was declared by the German government in February 1915. The declaration, which was approved by the Kaiser, assigned as a naval war zone the waters around Great Britain and Ireland, including the English Channel. Every enemy merchant ship found in that area by German U-boats would be destroyed, it was announced, whether or not it would be possible to avoid danger to the passengers and crew. Neutral ships navigating the war-zone waters, it was explained, would also be in danger of being sunk because of the misuse of neutral flags which it was alleged had been ordered by the British government. The water north of the Shetlands and a strip along the coast of Holland were left free to neutral ships.

When the German Ambassador, Count von Bernstorff, handed the declaration to Secretary of State Bryan on February 4, he stated that German naval forces had orders not to interfere with vessels that were clearly recognizable as neutrals, but advised that American vessels should avoid the war-zone waters. The Ambassador later commented that Mr. Bryan at first seemed to be incredulous, believing "a submarine campaign of this nature to be unthinkable."

The entire country, however, was not so incredulous as indignant, and the general protest the declaration aroused signified that if any vessel were sunk by a German submarine, involving the loss of American lives, the pressure of public opinion probably would result in a declaration of war by this country against Germany. President Wilson's reaction to the declaration came on February 12, when he caused Mr. Bryan to dispatch a note of protest to the German government. In this note he warned that if the commanders of German vessels of war "should destroy on the high seas an American ship or the lives of American citizens , , , the Government of the United

States would be constrained to hold the Imperial German Government to a strict accountability for such acts of their naval authorities," and to take any steps it might be necessary to take to safeguard the American lives and property, and to secure to American citizens the "full enjoyment of their acknowledged rights on the high seas."

* * *

"Out of the trenches and back to their homes by Christmas."

Henry Ford (1863-   )

WHILE THE United States feverishly engaged in preparedness for our inevitable entrance into the First World War, pacifists were ardently pleading and organizing for peace. Henry Ford, millionaire automobile manufacturer and consistent anti-militarist, was among the most earnest of the advocates of peace.

In December 1915 he chartered the steamer *Oscar II* and sent a peace delegation to Europe with the avowed purpose to get the soldiers "out of the trenches and back to their homes by Christmas."

The members of the delegation included many of fanatical and differing views and plans about how to achieve peace and the methods by which the speedy accomplishment of Mr. Ford's purpose was to be brought about were never clearly set forth.

At any rate the bickerings and antics aboard the *Oscar II* caused Mr. Ford to abandon the ship and the movement, which latter soon was laughed out of existence.

"Peace without victory."

[Thomas] Woodrow Wilson

EVEN AS the United States by the force of circumstances was being pushed, slowly but surely, toward involvement in World War 1, there was much discussion throughout the neutral world of some basis upon which the warring nations could agree to end the conflict. President Wilson on December 18, 1916, addressed an identical note to the belligerent governments, asking them to state the terms upon which they would deem it possible to make peace.

On January 22, 1917, he addressed the Senate to disclose the substance of the replies to his note and to inform the Senators, his constitutional advisers, of "the thought and purpose" that had been taking form in his own mind in regard to the duty of our Government in the days to come. He then stated in detail the principles which should be adopted by a League for Peace which he proposed.

He had been assured by both groups of belligerents, he stated, that it was no part of their purpose to crush their antagonists, that they did not seek to establish a balance of power in Europe. That the implication of these assurances might be equally clear "on both sides of the water," he gave his own understanding of what they were.

"They imply, first of all," he said, "that it must be a peace without victory."

Putting his own interpretation of this, he added: "Victory would mean peace forced upon the loser, a victor's terms imposed upon the vanquished. It would be accepted in humiliation, under duress, at an intolerable sacrifice, and would leave a sting, a resentment, a bitter memory upon which terms of peace would rest, not permanently . . . only a peace between equals can last."

"Every man in the draft age must work or fight."
Enoch Herbert Crowder (1859-   )

THE INITIAL enrollment of men of draft age under the Selective Service law of 1917 in the First World War totaled in excess of nine and a half million. After the first draft was made from this lot, many men were left in "deferred classification," and in November of that year the General Staff decided to classify the men not already drafted.

The work of formulating rules to govern draft boards in certifying numbers on calls by departments was assigned to the Provost Marshal General of the Army, Enoch H. Crowder. In issuing these rules Crowder instructed the boards:

"We shall give the idlers and the men not effectively employed the choice between military service and effective employment. Every man in the draft age, at least, must work or fight."

In the class of idlers were specified those who had no jobs or who made their living by gambling, clairvoyance, in bucket-shops, and on race tracks. Men said to be in "non-useful" occupations were: waiters, passenger elevator operators, footmen, domestic servants, clerks, and professional ball players. Men so employed, instead of having the deferred classification they would otherwise be entitled to because of age or domestic responsibilites, were to be put immediately in Class I.

"The world must be made safe for democracy."

[Thomas] Woodrow Wilson

THE MEMORABLE address in which this famous sentence was used contained several others only less celebrated. The occasion was the appearance of President Woodrow Wilson before the special session of the Congress on April 2, 1917, to recommend that the United States declare war against Germany. It was generally accepted that war would not long be delayed following the dismissal in February of the German Ambassador, Count von Bernstorff, upon his notification to this government of Germany's intention to resume unrestricted submarine warfare. The sinking without warning of the Cunard liner *Laconia,* with the loss of two American lives, the day after Wilson's second inauguration, made open war between the two countries almost inevitable, and the President called a special session of the Congress to convene on April 2. In his address the President, after citing the numerous outrages of Germany upon American lives and property, said:

"I advise that the Congress declare the recent course of the Imperial German Government to be, in fact, nothing less than war against the government and people of the United States; that it formally accept the status of belligerent which has been thrust upon it . . ."

After stating, as he said to make it clear to the world, what our motives and our objects were, the President continued: "We are now about to accept the gauge of battle with this natural foe to liberty, and shall, if necessary, spend the whole force of the nation to check and nullify its pretensions and its power. . . . The world must be made safe for democracy."

Elsewhere in his address the President declared: "The right is more precious than peace, and we shall fight for the things which we have always carried nearest our hearts,—for democracy, for the right of those who submit to authority to have a voice in their own govern-

ment, for the rights and liberties of small nations, for
a universal dominion of right by such a concert of free
peoples as shall bring peace and safety to all nations, and
make the world itself at last free."

* * *

"It's Heaven, Hell or Hoboken."

(1917)

MANY THOUSANDS of American boys of the millions in
the first world war probably had never heard of Hoboken
up to the time of their induction into the American Ex-
peditionary Force. There was no special reason why they
should have known of it, for although it was an important
community in several ways apart from the military use
made of it, it was only one of several small towns in
New Jersey on the west bank of the Hudson River across
from New York City.

Yet Hoboken was to loom large in their lives, for it
was the gateway to their service abroad, to new and
strange experiences, to a fate that was hidden in the mists
of the future. Hoboken was the great port of embarkation
for our troops sent overseas, and also the port that received them on their return from foreign service. Hence
it became in their minds a symbol of a happy termination
of their service, and the phrase, "It's Heaven, Hell or
Hoboken," expressed the somewhat fatalistic thought that
escape from death in battle, with consequent reward or
punishment in the hereafter, meant a return via Hoboken
to peace-time life.

Albert Jay Cook in his verses, "Heaven, Hell or Hoboken," published in *Stars and Stripes*, the A.E.F.'s war-time
publication, made the expression generally familiar.

"Food Will Win the War."

(1917)

THE EXTRAORDINARY importance that food assumes in time of war was made apparent in the United States very soon after we entered World War I. Out of our abundance we had been able to ship vast quantities abroad, where normal agricultural production had been interfered with by shortages of labor caused by the drafting of men into the armies. To the average person, the war did not seem to present any great problem in the way of providing food sufficient for our own population and the peoples abroad who were in need of it. To those responsible for the conduct of the war, however, the problem was real.

The first effort to solve it was the formation in May 1917, of a voluntary Food Administration, of which President Wilson appointed Herbert C. Hoover chief. Hoover had been in Europe at the outbreak of the war and was little known except as a successful mining engineer and an able business administrator. He had been appointed chief of the Commission for Relief in Belgium and had become internationally known because of his efficient work in that capacity. After this country became involved in the European war he had said that "the foremost duty of America toward the Allies in this war is to see that they are supplied with food."

Hoover's appointment as head of the voluntary Food Administration was followed by organized propaganda directed to impressing upon the American public the importance in war of adequate food supplies, and the slogan, "Food Will Win the War," became a rallying cry. The necessity of raising food and of conserving it was emphasized and instructions were published as to the right sorts of food to be saved and shipped, and how to derive the maximum value from the foods available for domestic consumption. In the interest of conserving the available supplies of grains, meat, and sugar, there were "wheatless", "meatless,", and "sweetless" days when these items were supposed to be omitted from meals either in the homes or public eating places.

The voluntary Food Administration was succeeded by one established under the Food Control law and Hoover was appointed Food Administrator.

* * *

"We must be the great arsenal of democracy."
Franklin Delano Roosevelt

THE RE-ELECTION in 1940 of Franklin D. Roosevelt to a a second term was followed not long after by a bolder move than he had theretofore made toward action "short of War." This country had not yet been drawn into the second World War, but its neutrality was no more than nominal and it was realized generally that it was only a matter of time until all pretense of being neutral would be thrown aside.

The Lend-Lease Act that was to end definitely our neutrality was foreshadowed in the President's fireside talk from the White House on Sunday evening, December 29, 1940. In this talk to the nation the President said:

"We must be the great arsenal of democracy. For us this is an emergency as serious as war itself. We must apply ourselves to our task with the same resolution, the same sense of urgency, the same spirit of patriotism and sacrifice as we would show were we at war. . . ."

On January 6, 1941, the President sent his annual message to the Congress in which he recommended the enactment of a Lend-Lease Bill.

"A bridge of ships."

A FEW days after the United States declared war against Germany, David Lloyd George, Prime Minister of Great Britain, in a talk at the American Luncheon Club in London, said that "The road to victory, the guaranty of victory, the absolute assurance of victory, has to be found in one word, ships in a second word, ships, and a third word, ships." There was good reason for his statement. Germany's submarines were sinking the Allies' merchant-men faster than their yards could launch new bottoms. In the second quarter of 1917, that in which Lloyd George spoke, England alone lost 1,360,000 tons of merchant ships, swelling the grand total to 5,360,000 tons since the beginning of the war. About the time of the Prime Minister's address, Edward N. Hurley, chairman of the United States Shipping Board, estimated that "one out of every four ships leaving the United Kingdom for overseas" never returned.

"A bridge of ships" to win the war became a popular slogan in the United States. The Government had foreseen that an opportunity to win the war lay in building ships faster than the submarines could sink them. Ten days after the declaration of war the Emergency Fleet Corporation, a subsidiary of the Shipping Board, was chartered to provide the "bridge of ships" over which a constant supply of men and materials should pass from this country to the battlefields overseas. The Shipping Board announced that it would requisition three million tons deadweight of ships and would build fifteen million tons more. To carry out the building programme all shipyards in the country were utilized and many new ones authorized, and ships of wood, steel and even concrete were ordered. Even though the program, especially as it related to the construction of steel ships, was never fully carried out, a real contribution to the war effort was made.

"The 'bridge of ships' slogan was reminiscent of the prior use made of a somewhat similar phrase. When the steamer *Sirius* arrived in New York's harbor on April 23, 1838, having made the crossing from Cork, Ireland, in seventeen days, James Gordon Bennett's New York *Herald* enthusiastically announced: "The Broad Atlantic Bridged At Last."

* * *

"They [the Germans] can go to hell."

Charles White Whittlesey (1884-1921)

ONE OF the stirring episodes of the American army's campaign in France in the first World War was the gallant fight of the "Lost Battalion" commanded by Major Charles W. Whittlesey. For five days this detachment, the First Battalion of the 308th Infantry and elements of both the 307th and 306th Infantry Machine Gun Battalion of the 77th (New York) Division, was hemmed in at the bottom of a ravine by Germans in the Meuse-Argonne battle of October 1918.

The battalion was not really "lost" but was isolated in its position one and a half miles northeast of Binarville. Its situation was desperate and seemed hopeless, but despite heavy casualties Whittlesey refused refeated demands that he surrender. To a written demand carried to him under a flag of truce he gave the bearer a verbal refusal which was understood by his men at the time to consist in the defiant answer that the Germans "Can go to hell."* The battalion soon after was relieved by the 154th Brigade. Whittlesey received the Congressional Medal of Honor for his conduct on this occasion.

---

* Several years after the event Whittlesey, whose rank had been advanced to a lieutenant-colonelcy, told me that he had not given his answer to the German demand in the words popularly attributed to him. His recollection of the circumstance was that he had crumpled the written communication and thrown it to the ground, muttering: "They can go to hell."—H. F. W.

"Force, Force to the utmost."

[*Thomas*] *Woodrow Wilson*

PRESIDENT WILSON'S forbearance in the face of repeated provocations by Germany in World War I was regarded variously by his countrymen. By those whose pro-Ally sympathies were pronounced and who favored the entrance of this country into the war against Germany, Wilson's course was considered to be ultra-pacifist and evidence of weakness. On the other hand, those who urged strict neutrality of this country lauded the President for "keeping us out of war."

Once the country had declared war on Germany, however, the President's attitude changed radically. His vigor of action and speech demonstrated the truth of the aphorism about the anger of a patient man, and was an inspiriting call to the patriotism of a nation at war. The long series of notes, logically and clearly phrased, with which he had sought to induce Germany to respect this country's rights as a neutral were succeeded by ringing public utterances that backed up the nation's military measures to meet the enemy's challenge.

A notable instance of the new temper of Wilson's speech was that of his address at a Liberty Loan rally in Baltimore on April 6, 1918. In that address he said:

"Germany has once more said that force and force alone shall decide whether Justice and Peace shall reign in the affairs of men, whether Right as America conceives it, shall determine the destinies of mankind. There is therefore but one response possible from us, Force, Force to the utmost, Force without stint or limit, the righteous and triumphant Force which shall make Peace the law of the world, and cast every selfish Dominion down in the dust."

"Forty Men, Eight Horses."

(1918)

THE SENSE of humor of the average American soldier that enabled him to make the best of an inconvenient situation was in evidence many times in the First World War. One of the best examples of this happy faculty was their reaction to the facilities provided by French railroads for the inland transport of troops. The box cars used for this bore the painted legend, "Hommes 40—Chevaux 8," indicating that the capacity of each car was forty men or eight horses.

The frankly alternative nature of these cars was diverting to most of the American soldiers, although the experience of riding in them was more or less an ordeal. For it is the testimony of those who had the experience that, however ample the space might be for horses, the average American doughboy's bulk was such as to preclude comfort in thus traveling in company with thirty-nine others of his comrades.

In retrospect, however, the discomforts of this way of travel seem to have been forgotten by veterans of the A.E.F., who after the war remembered principally its humors. After the American Legion was organized they formed La Societe des 40 Hommes et 8 Chevaux, or as it is better known to Legionnaires, the Forty and Eight Society. The society was founded as a playground of the Legion and in its heyday numbered more than fifty thousand members within the Legion's roster. Until their initiation new members are known as "Poor Goofs," thereafter as "Voyageurs Militaire." The flavor of their experiences in France is further preserved in the titles by which the State and local branches and the officers are known. The branches are called "voitures"; the head of the society, "Chef de Chemin de Fer"; and the six vice presidents, "Sous Chefs de Chemin de Fer."

"We have sought no shooting war with Hitler."

Franklin Delano Roosevelt

As WORLD WAR II entered into its third year, the activities of German submarines increased and their depredations included the ships of belligerent and neutral countries alike.

On September 4, 1941, the United States destroyer *Greer* while carrying mail to the American outpost in Iceland was attacked in full daylight by a German submarine off the southeast coast of Greeland. Two torpedoes were fired at the destroyer, which was flying the American flag.

President Roosevelt in his "fireside talk" of September 11 said of the *Greer* incident that it "was piracy—legally and morally." Prefacing a recital of prior attacks and sinkings of neutral vessels by German submarines, he said that "Attack has followed attack."

He told of the torpedoing and sinking of the American flag merchant ship, the *Robin Moor,* in the South Atlantic; of an attempted attack by a submarine on an American battleship in North Atlantic waters; and of the sinkings near Greenland of an American-owned ship flying the flag of the Republic of Panama, and of the United States merchant ship *Steel Seafarer* in the Red Sea.

These acts of international lawlessness, the President stated, were a manifestation of the Nazi design "to abolish the freedom of the seas, and to acquire absolute control and domination of the sea for themselves."

Hitler knew, the President said, that to be ultimately successful in world mastery he must get control of the seas, first destroying "the bridge of ships we are building across the Atlantic, over which we shall continue to roll the implements of war to help destroy him and all his work in the end."

The attack on the *Greer,* he characterized as a "determined step towards creating a permanent world system based on force, terror and murder."

Acts of violence or intimidation, he asserted, would be ineffective to prevent this country from keeping intact its two bulwarks of defense: our line of supply of material to Hitler's enemies, and the freedom of our shipping on the high seas. Regardless of what the cost might be, he added, this course would be maintained.

"We have sought no shooting war with Hitler," he declared. "We do not seek it now. But neither do we want peace so much, that we are willing to pay for it by permitting him to attack our naval and merchant ships while they are on legitimate business."

* * *

"Praise the Lord and pass the ammunition."

Howell Maurice Forgy (1908-)

WHEN JAPANESE war planes descended on Pearl Harbor on Sunday morning December 7, 1941, Howell M. Forgy, Chaplain U.S.N., lay in his bunk aboard the United States cruiser *New Orleans* in the harbor. As the planes loosed their bombs upon the naval vessels and the fortifications the *New Orleans'* guns went into action.

While the line of sweating sailors labored at the shell hoists below decks the chaplain stood by watching the men handle the heavy projectiles, encouraging them with the oft-repeated exhortation, "Praise the Lord and pass the ammunition."

The chaplain's phrase became current in the Navy and soon afterward was the subject of a popular song.

"A date which will live in infamy."

Franklin Delano Roosevelt

THE INDIGNATION and outraged feeling of the American
people at the treacherous attack on Pearl Harbor were
voiced by President Roosevelt in the very beginning of
his message to the Congress asking that a state of war be
declared to exist between the United States and the Japanese Empire.

"Yesterday, December 7, 1941—a date which will live
in infamy—" the message began, "the United States of
America was suddenly and deliberately attacked by naval
and air forces of the Empire of Japan."

The President's message was brief; recounting the diplomatic conversations between the ambassadors of Japan
and this government, which continued to the very hour
of the bombing of Pearl Harbor, the President said that
it was "obvious that the attack was deliberately planned
many days or even weeks" before it was made. After
enumerating the attacks by the Japanese successively on
Malaya, Hong Kong, Guam, the Philippines, Wake Island,
and Midway Island, all made within twenty-four hours'
time, the President declared:

"Always will we remember the character of the onslaught against us."

"This phony war."

(1939)

COMPARATIVE INACTION succeeded the sudden and swift conquest of Poland by the German *blitzkrieg* in World War II. With the Polish armies overwhelmed and scattered, their capital battered and in ruins, their entire country overrun and occupied by the invaders, Germany's armies rested before their next onslaught upon the Western powers.

The French armies awaited them behind the Maginot Line, putting their trust in its supposed impregnability and in a strategy of defense. England was not yet ready and was feverishly arming. The United States stood aloof and a policy of strict neutrality on the part of this country was strongly advocated by many, among whom the most prominent was Senator William E. Borah, of Idaho, chairman of the Senate Foreign Relations Committee from 1925 to 1934. As the most powerful spokesman of the isolationist segment of the Nation, Senator Borah led the opposition to President Roosevelt's recommendation to the special session of the Seventy-sixth Congress, which convened on September 21, 1939, that the Neutrality Act be revised to abolish the embargo on the shipment of munitions to belligerents and to establish the cash-and carry system instead.

While the debate on the recommendation was on, many critics with isolationist sympathies regarded with suspicion the lull in military operations overseas. Despite the conquest of Poland with its accompanying devastation of that country, the war in Europe was characterized as "This phony war," especially by those who had not favored the intervention of the Western powers in Poland's behalf.

"There are no atheists in the fox holes."

William Thomas Cummings (1903-   )

BATAAN WILL ever be a name to evoke in Americans sentiments of pity, pride, and admiration. Perhaps not since the awful winter of Valley Forge has any body of American soldiers been called on to endure the ordeal suffered by the outnumbered American and Filipino troops on Bataan in the five months they held out after the Japanese attack on Pearl Harbor, December 7, 1941. Half starved, famished, weakened by disease and hunger, bombed daily by Japanese planes against which there were no American planes to rise, their pitifully small numbers steadily diminished by deaths and wounds, they fought on grimly.

Yet even as their hopes of relief faded and they knew the inevitable end, their morale remained unimpaired and as they fought they could sing the doggerel verse:

We're the battling bastards of Bataan;
No Mamma, No Papa, no Uncle Sam.

The indomitable spirit of the men was aided by the example of their officers who bore uncomplainingly the sufferings, misery, and filth that were the lot of the common soldier. Especially was their morale helped by the words and ministrations of their chaplains, one of whom, Father William T. Cummings, a Maryknoll mission priest, commissioned a first lieutenant, declared in a field sermon that "There are no atheists in the fox holes."

When Japanese planes bombed Base Hospital No. 1 on April 4, Father Cummings went among the sick and wounded men there, ministering to them and seeking to encourage them. Mounting a chair among them he led them in reciting the Lord's Prayer. He was struck by a fragment of shell but, with the blood streaming down his face from a wound in his uplifted arm, he continued to the end of the prayer. Only after the bombing had ceased

did he ask a nurse to apply a tourniquet to his arm to
stop the flow of blood.

When the fall of Bataan became imminent he was urged
by his superiors to escape to Corregidor, but he refused,
declaring, "I have a job to do." When Bataan surrendered
he was made prisoner by the Japanese and was among
those to make the dreadful "Death March" to a prison
camp.

*   *   *

"Sighted sub. Sank same."

David Francis Mason (1914-   )

LATE IN March 1942, the nation was thrilled and amused
at the laconic announcement of his victorious encounter
with a navy vessel of our Japanese foes by a young American. On that occasion David F. Mason, of Rochester,
Minnesota, chief aviation machinist's mate, U.S.N., flying
on a routine patrol over the South Pacific, discerned a
Japanese submarine which had surfaced.

Mason swooped his plane over the craft and dropped
several depth charges. Very soon there was an explosion,
and the wreckage of the submarine was strewn over the
water. Mason resumed his patrol and radioed his base.

"Sighted sub. Sank same."

For his feat he was awarded the Silver Star. He had
already won the Distinguished Flying Cross for sinking a
Japanese submarine in the same waters. This was on
February 26, 1942, when as a machinist's mate flying a
Navy plane, he noticed the wake of a submarine which
was submerged to periscope depth. He dived, dropped
two bombs, and sank the craft.

"I shall return."

Douglas MacArthur (1880-   )

WITHIN TWO years and a little more than seven months of the day he left the Philippines for Australia, General Douglas MacArthur had taken the first step toward the fulfillment of the promise he made at the time of his departure.

"I shall return," he assured fellow officers and friends when on the night of March 11, 1942, he boarded a small patrol boat for the 3,000-mile voyage to Australia. When he left the islands it was as commander of all the United States forces in the Far East. When he waded ashore with his troops to invade the island of Leyte on October 19, 1944, it was as Commander in Chief of the unified forces in the Eastern Pacific. The landing on Leyte was followed in succession by another on Mindoro, and the invasion of northern Luzon, whence MacArthur's army marched south on Manila. On February 7 MacArthur and his staff entered Manila.

Very soon after Pearl Harbor, MacArthur realized that with the forces available to him, and lacking adequate coverage from the air, he could not hold all the beaches of the Philippines. On Christmas Eve he and his staff left Manila for Corregidor, the rock fort on Manila Bay, to make a stand against the Japanese. Two days later Manila was declared an open city, despite which it was bombed by Japanese planes. On January 2, the city was surrendered to the Japanese. As the fall of Corregidor became inevitable, President Roosevelt ordered Mac-Arthur to leave the Rock and proceed to Australia where he was to establish headquarters. Reluctantly, he turned over the command to Lieutenant General Jonathan M. Wainwright. Six days later he was in Melbourne whither he had been flown by airplane to which he transferred from the small boat in which he had departed from Corregidor.

In Melbourne he repeated the pledge given in Corregidor. "I came through and I shall return," he said.

Bataan and Corregidor fell, and MacArthur's long and arduous struggle to return to the Philippines began. One of his objectives, the liberation of American prisoners held by the Japanese in the islands, was realized in part when on January 30, 1945, a band of 407 American Rangers and Filipino guerrillas rescued 513 prisoners of war. The Rangers, led by Lieutenant Colonel Henry Mucci, and the guerillas, under the command of Major Robert Lapham, in a night march penetrated twenty-five miles behind the Japanese lines in East Luzon and in a surprise attack on the Cabanatuan prison camp near Cabu killed all the Japanese guards and liberated 486 Americans, survivors of the "Death March" of Bataan; twenty-three British, three Netherlanders, and one Norwegian.

The return march of the rescuers was made under furious attack by the Japanese, led by tanks, but the Japanese were fought off with a loss of 523 of their men killed. Twenty-seven of the rescuing force were killed. Although in a pitably weakened condition from malnutrition, hunger, disease, and unhealed wounds, all except two of the rescued prisoners were brought back in safety to the American lines. Two men died when their weakened hearts were unequal to the strain of their liberation.

"We took a hell of a beating."

Joseph Warren Stillwell (1883-   )

IN THE early stages of the war with Japan the expedition in Burma of American, British, and Chinese forces ended disastrously for the Allies.

Lieutenant General Joseph W. Stilwell, of the United States Army, had been put in command of the Chinese Fifth and Sixth Armies by Generalissimo Chiang Kai-shek of China, and operated in Burma in conjunction with British forces.

The Allied armies were unable to make headway against the Japanese, due in great part to the lack of air support, whereas the Japanese were well supplied in this particular, having an estimated number of five hundred planes in the air against the Allies. Mandalay was abandoned by the British and Chinese forces on May 1, 1942 and steadily the Allied armies were pushed northward.

Evacuation of Burma and withdrawal to India became inevitable, and by the latter part of May, it was announced that virtually all British troops had been withdrawn from Burma.

Stilwell had made a plan, which was approved of, to bring his Chinese troops out of Burma to India, but countermanding orders from China caused confusion and costly losses. He began his retreat, on May 17, at the head of a small force of Americans, British, Chinese, and Burmese, including women army nurses. The march to India was mostly afoot, as bad roads necessitated the abandonment of their motor transport. For 200 miles the little party trudged wearily through a cholera-infested and malaria-ridden terrain of mountains, jungle, and swamps, wading rivers, existing on meagre rations, and doing never less than nine, sometimes twenty-four, miles a day, and always with the pursuing Japanese forces only two days' march behind them. Yet discipline was never relaxed, and Stilwell shared with his men all the hardships of the journey, refusing to ride and ordering that the horses were for the use of the women in the party only.

After six or seven days of this grueling march the little band reached India. Although the failure of the Burmese expedition was a great disappointment to Stilwell, he had no excuse to make for it, merely commenting: "The Japs ran us out of Burma. We took a hell of a beating."

Stilwell spoke Chinese fluently and had a high regard for his native troops, to whom he was known as "General Sze," and whom he considered as man for man superior to Japanese soldiers.

His comment on the disastrous outcome of the campaign was characteristic of his informality of speech and forceful plain-speaking, which caused him to be known among American troops as "the shirt-sleeves general," "Uncle Joe," and Vinegar Joe."

* * *

"A hell of a way to make a living."

(1944)

MORALISTS AND philosophers from time immemorial have expatiated on the folly and futility of war. Perhaps none of them has so well summed up the case against the business of waging war as the sententious remark of an American private soldier in the thick of battle. As told by W. C. Heinz, correspondent of the New York *Sun,* writing of the campaign around Aachen in the summer of 1944, he sought shelter from artillery fire during a severe engagement on the outskirts of the German town of Stolberg. The correspondent made for a foxhole whose occupant, an anonymous American infantryman, rolled away to make room for him, remarking: "This is a hell of a way to make a living, isn't it?"

"Pick out the biggest one and fire."

Edward Joseph Moran (1894-   )

THE NAVAL battle off Cape Esperance in the Solomons Island on the night of October 11-12, 1942, in one respect was unique in our war with Japan. In that engagement a single American war vessel took on six of the enemy and bore the brunt of the battle in which they were destroyed. Outnumbered and outgunned, the United States light cruiser *Boise* sank five Japanese men-of-war and helped destroy a sixth.

An American task force had been sent to prevent enemy landings on Guadalcanal and lay in wait for them off Cape Esperance. The *Boise*, Captain Edward J. ("Mike") Moran commanding, late at night sighted six Japanese warships steaming in two parallel columns, one of which was composed of larger ships than those in the other. The *Boise* advanced between the columns and Captain Moran gave the order:

"Pick out the biggest one and fire."

The *Boise's* main batteries were laid on a heavy Japanese cruiser in the lead, and her anti-aircraft fire was directed at the smaller vessels. The Japanese cruiser was soon disposed of, and in succession the *Boise* destroyed four other warships. The sixth enemy ship was sunk with the aid of the fire from other vessels of the task force.

In all, the enemy lost in this action one heavy cruiser, four destroyers and a transport. The *Boise* had fired 1000 rounds of five-inch and six-inch shells, but was hit repeatedly by the damaging eight-inch armament of the Japanese. Badly crippled, at one time the *Boise* was in flames but Moran ordered her magazines flooded and the ship was saved. She was given up for lost by the others of the task force, but the next day succeeded in rejoining them.

The Navy Cross was awarded to Captain Moran for his gallant handling of the *Boise* and later he was advanced in rank to Commodore.

"Take her down!"

Howard W. Gilmore (1903-1943)

FAITHFUL TO the traditions of the Navy, the commander of an American submarine in the war with Japan chose death that his vessel and its crew might be saved. The submarine, whose skipper was Commander Howard W. Gilmore, operating in South Pacific waters, had been a terror to Japanese shipping, and on a night in February 1943 had sunk one Japanese merchantman and badly crippled another.

A Japanese gunboat hurried to the scene and attempted to ram the submarine, which had surfaced, but Gilmore evaded it, rammed the gunboat instead and sundered its plates. The gunboat, though sinking remained afloat and poured a furious fire on the crew above decks. Gilmore was struck by a bullet and mortally wounded. Out of reach of the hatch and of his men and realizing that he was dying and that an attempt to lower him through the hatch would cause delay and endanger the submarine and its crew, Gilmore commanded:

"Take her down!"

The order was obeyed, the submarine submerged, and her gallant commander was washed into the sea and perished.

Not until the Navy Department in February 1945, announced the loss of the U.S.S. *Growler*, commanded by Gilmore's successor, Commander Thomas B. Oakley, who with his crew was lost, was the name of the vessel saved by Gilmore made known. The Congressional Medal of Honor was awarded to Gilmore posthumously. He had already received the Navy Cross for sinking two Japanese destroyers and damaging a third in the enemy's own harbor, and the Gold Cross for sinking 24,946 tons of enemy shipping.

"For the duration."

(*1942-*   )

IT WAS a novel experience for Americans, during the war with Japan, not to be able to buy the goods and services they had been purchasing theretofore without let or hindrance. Persistent advertising urging them, not only to buy certain articles, but also to call for them by their brand names, had created a demand that was always readily supplied.

When the country's manufacturing system was put on a war basis, however, and the manufacture of the less essential goods used by civilians was either curtailed or abandoned altogether, or they were diverted almost entirely to the use of our armed forces, the pinch was felt acutely by civilian consumers.

The explanation given by retailers for the increasing shortages or stoppages of articles was succinct: "Discontinued (or scarce) for the duration of the war." In time it was stereotyped into the briefer phrase, "For the duration." It was not only a valid excuse, but also an apt reminder that as the nation's manhood had been drafted into its armed service "for the duration," it was only just that civilians should accept uncomplainingly the minor deprivations and inconveniences incident to war.

It was accepted in that spirit generally, and the phrase became current also as a joking explanation for a variety of departures from the normal. Furthermore, as illustrative of the belief that normal conditions could not be expected immediately upon the cessation of war, a favorite remark was that of the man who observed: "I'm afraid this here duration's going to last a long time after the war."

"We will let the rest ripen on the vine."

[William] Frank[lin] Knox (1874-1944)

WHEN THE land and sea forces of the United States had recovered from the treacherous blow dealt by the Japanese at Pearl Harbor and were beginning their sure and gradual advance upon Japan some dissatisfaction was expressed by civilians at a phase of naval strategy. This was the policy of what was called "island hopping," that is, the bombing and invasion of certain islands in the Pacific held by the Japanese, while by-passing others.

An important operation of this kind was the bombing and invasion of the Marshall Islands in January and February 1943, a co-ordinated sea, air, and land power operation which was preceded by the shelling of Kwajalein and Roi in the Marshalls group by naval forces under the over-all command of Admiral Chester W. Nimitz, with Vice Admiral Raymond A. Spruance in immediate command.

This operation, Secretary of the Navy Frank Knox told a press conference in Washington on February 11, 1944, was significant as a pretty good denial of the "arm-chair strategists' bugaboo, island hopping."

"We have hopped on them [the Japanese]," he said, "in selected places and will let the rest of them ripen on the vine. Eventually they will die of starvation."

The Secretary's phrase, which was oftener quoted as "wither on the vine," assumed added point when early in 1945 estimates of the number of Japanese on the by-passed islands were published. One estimate placed the total at 250,000 in garrisons cut off from contact with the homeland, their holdings no longer having strategic value, with diminished supplies which they were unable to replace regularly, and subject to bombing and eventual capture or annihilation by the American forces.

"Don't you know there's a war on?"

(1942-1943)

UNTIL THE attack on Pearl Harbor Americans as a people were only dimly conscious that the mightiest war in the world's history was being fought. They knew, of course, that the German hordes had invaded, conquered, and overrun most of Europe and were dealing staggering blows to a sore-beset Great Britain, but the war as yet had not touched this nation and, so thought many, might never reach it. Americans had experienced almost none of the hardships, discomforts, and inconveniences that were every day the common lot of the peoples engaged in the struggle. They knew, indeed, that there was a war on, but it was remote.

The entrance of the United States into a war on two fronts in Europe and in Asia, brought this experience to Americans, not suddenly, but gradually. In a land of wealth, of plenty, of vast resources, shortages of goods, supplies, and services developed as war became the business of the nation and its peace-time economy gave way to a war economy. Regimentation, rationing of the necessities of life, mounting taxes, increased prices, and a steadily declining standard of living shortened the tempers and lowered the spirits of a people harassed and worried, and the daily iteration of the sarcastic question, "Don't you know there's a war on?" became in many instances an excuse to cover the inefficiency, indifference, and lack of courtesy of some retailers or those paid to render services of various kinds. As a retort to even the mildest complaint it became in time so irritating as to cause violence on some occasions.

The implication in the question, that the American people were complacent and didn't realize that we were at war and that the fact entailed some curtailment of our comfort and convenience, was refuted by a soldier returning to the front from furlough.

"That's a crock of stew," was his slangy comment. "The people at home know the score."

* * *

"It gets them [the Italians] to third base."
Ellery Wheeler Stone (1894-)

As a conquered nation, the government of Italy in World War II for a time was administered by an Allied Commission. Gradually as the American and British armies advanced northward on the peninsula and liberated towns and cities from German possession, control was given to the Italians themselves. After the liberation of Rome an Italian government was organized under the premiership of Ivanoe Bonomi, an anti fascist statesman.

In March 1945, control of Italy south of a line extending across the peninsula fifty miles north of Rome was turned over to the Bonomi government by the Allied Commission. Necessarily, this control was not unlimited, for as long as German forces continued to hold some of the richest and most populous parts of Italy checks on military and naval matters had to be reserved to the Allies.

That this naturally fell short of the desires of the Italian government and people was recognized by Ellery Stone, chief commissioner, who commented that still "It gets them to third base."

"Nuts!"

Anthony Clement McAuliffe (1898-   )

In Victor Hugo's description of the Battle of Waterloo
he devotes an entire chapter in *Les Miserables* to a glorifi-
cation of the reply, in a single word, made by a French
officer to a demand for his surrender. An American officer,
Brigadier General Anthony C. McAuliffe, was similarly
laconic when called on by the Germans to surrender after
McAuliffe's outnumbered troops had stubbornly held
their position in Bastogne, Belgium, in Von Runstedt's
drive through Belgium in December 1944.

McAuliffe was in command of the 101st Airborne Division at Bastogne, an important position in the path of
the German break-through which began on December 16.
From December 19 to 22, McAuliffe's troops withstood
repeated fierce assaults on their position. On the latter
date a German officer was sent to the perimeter of the
American defense with a formal demand for their surrender.

McAuliffe's response to the demand was the scornful
word "Nuts!", and an American officer was sent with it
to the waiting German. As reported by the Associated
Press, the German emissary asked:

"Is your commander's reply favorable? If it is I am
empowered to continue negotiation of terms."

"My commander's reply is 'Nuts' " the American told
him.

"What does that mean?" the puzzled German inquired.

"It means, 'Go to hell,' " was the answer.

The German officer understood that, saluted stiffly, and
marched off.

The German forces, consisting of elements of seven
divisions, resumed the battle, which culminated in an
attack on Christmas morning. But Bastogne never was
surrendered.

For his gallant defense of Bastogne McAuliffe was advanced to the rank of Major General.

* * *

"The Yankee Bean Pot."

(1945)

ONE OF the most effective weapons of destruction devised by the chemical experts of this country in our war with Japan was the M-69 incendiary bomb first used early in 1945. In March of that year many tons of these bombs were rained down by American planes upon the great Japanese cities of Tokyo, Nagoya, Nagasaki, and Kobe, as well as upon other communities of Japan's homeland. The devastation wrought by them was so great as to cause the admission by the Japanese government that the nation was in a critical situation.

These deadly bombs were first put into mass production in New England plants, and this circumstance led the New York *Sun* to suggest editorially that the M-69 might appropriately be dubbed the "Yankee Bean Pot."

As described by the Chemical War Service, the bomb consists of six-pound missiles gathered into an "aimable" cluster of 500-pound weight. When dropped from the plane, the cluster opens at a set altitude, and the component bombs are released. Each bomb is filled with jellied gasoline and when it is exploded the burning fluid is thrown for about thirty yards around the point of contact.

The "Yankee Bean Pot" was especially designed for use against the highly inflammable Japanese targets, and the burned-out areas in Japan's large cities attested their deadly effectiveness.

"With ten minutes to spare."

(1945)

HISTORY RECORDS few instances of a great military success achieved with so scant a margin of time as that by which American troops seized the great Ludendorff bridge across the Rhine in the final stages of the second world war in Germany. After General von Runstedt's breakthrough in Belgium, in December 1944, had been stopped and the German forces had been pushed back across the Rhine, the Allied forces in the latter part of February began a great offfensive which swept the German armies before them and resulted in the fall of Cologne.

To press their advantage, it was all important for the Allies to cross the Rhine, but the bridges at Cologne had been destroyed, as had been most of the others across that historic stream. While General Patton's Third Army pushed northwards, elements of General Hodges' First Army raced southward from Cologne to seize the Ludendorff bridge at Remagen, which was still standing. The Germans had concentrated their forces in an effort to stop Patton, with the result that the attack on Remagen was a tactical surprise and met with little resistance from the weakened forces there.

Hodges' men arrived at the place late in the afternoon and learned from German prisoners that demolition charges has been placed on the bridge and that its destruction had been set for 4 o'clock that afternoon. With only ten minutes to spare a platoon was dispatched to the bridge to remove the explosives and save the bridge. As they approached, a German watchman in the bridge tower pulled a switch, setting off the first charge, which did only slight immediate damage. The German then fled, and without delay the Americans ripped out all the wires connected with the demolition charges. The bridge was saved temporarily, and soon American troops, tanks, artillery armament, and materiel were pouring across it to establish a bridgehead at its eastern end. American troops were the first invaders of the Rhineland since Napoleon's armies in 1805.

* * *

"There's no future in it."

(1945)

"FAILED TO RETURN" was a laconic official epitaph on war planes lost in World War II. The tremendous part played by the air services in bringing about the subjugation of the enemy countries was every day made apparent by the communiques on the operations on all fronts on both hemispheres. As the war lengthened and many thousands of planes were put into service for the overwhelming of the enemy the losses suffered by our air forces increased proportionately and the cost in the nation's young manhood was very great.

The chances of survival for the personnel of a plane shot down in combat or by anti-aircraft fire were not considered by aviators to be many, but these courageous young men developed a resigned, if not fatalistic attitude toward the risks. If not death, then capture. And if the latter should be by the Japanese, death by torture or slow starvation was the almost certain prospect. Any way the aviator's fighting career was viewed, it seemed to offer few, if any, happy alternatives.

"There's no future in it," was the grimly humorous phrase in which they summed up their estimate of it.

PART THREE

SOCIOLOGICAL—ECONOMIC
COMMERCIAL

"Not worth a continental."

(1790)

AT THE end of the War of the Revolution the government was virtually bankrupt. Large sums of money were owing to France and Holland, and the interest on these debts was in arrears. Congress could not raise money sufficient for the needs of government or for servicing the debt because it had no power to provide revenue by taxation nor could it require the States to contribute to the national treasury. Its only recourse was to issue paper money, called "continental currency."

This had been done in the amount of $200,000,000, which had shrunk in value so rapidly that it took $40 in this paper to buy a dollar in silver. The contempt in which this currency was held was reflected in the popular phrase expressive of its worthlessness.

"He touched the dead corpse of Public Credit, and it sprang upon its feet."

Daniel Webster

FORTY YEARS after Alexander Hamilton, the first Secretary of the Treasury, had set the young nation upon its feet financially, Webster pronounced his eulogy: "He smote the rock of the national resources, and abundant streams of revenue gushed forth. He touched the dead corpse of Public Credit, and it sprang upon its feet." The occasion was a public dinner given in New York March 10, 1831, in honor of Webster.

When Hamilton became Secretary of the Treasury the national debt was $54,000,000, more than $10,000,000 of which was owed to French and Dutch bankers, and the balance a domestic debt. The latter was in the form of promissory notes pledging the government to pay the holder the amount named on the face of the note. Speculators had bought up many of these notes which had fallen far below their par value.

There was general agreement throughout the nation that the national debt in so far as it affected foreign creditors should be paid, but Hamilton's proposal to redeem the domestic notes at their full face value was vigorously opposed. Hamilton, however, not only insisted that the United States keep faith with all its creditors, but that the national government assume the debts, amounting to some $20,000,000, incurred by the several states in the Revolutionary war. His policies prevailed, with what success history records.

"Law is whatever is boldly asserted and plausibly maintained."

Aaron Burr (1756-1836)

A ROMANTIC and sinister figure in his country's history, Aaron Burr was yet a man of distinguished qualities of mind, an able politician, and a brilliant practitioner of law. The man who had missed being President by the margin of one vote, became instead Vice President and while in that office killed in a duel Alexander Hamilton, his one-time fellow officer in the Continental Army, and later his opponent in politics and rival in the practice of law. Finally, all hopes of a continuance of a political career was ended for him by his trial and acquittal on a charge of treason.

Understandably, Burr at times was cynical in his views and comments. Perhaps the most notable of several legal maxims attributed to him was the opinion he expressed that, "Law is whatever is boldly asserted and plausibly maintained."

"All's Set!"

(*1820*)

THE ESTABLISHMENT of the Santa Fe Trail early in the nineteenth century opened the great Southwest to an ever increasing stream of emigrants from the country east of the Mississippi River. By the beginning of the second quarter of the century the era of the covered wagon had set in and until the coming of the railroads the plains of Kansas at the border of the trail's eastern end at Independence, Missouri, and the country beyond were traversed by thousands of wagons bearing pioneers and their families and great stores of goods to be exchanged in trade with the Spanish settlers in New Mexico. Frequently the wagon trains were escorted by small bodies of troops as a protection against the raids of hostile Indians. The teamsters' shout, "All's set," as they cracked their whips, was the signal for the setting out on the journey by the trains, some of which numbered as many as a hundred wagons, drawn by teams of ten or twelve mules or oxen.

"The Tariff of Abominations."

(1828)

PRIOR TO Henry Clay's advocacy of the "American System" of protectionism, customs duties on imports into this country had been levied mainly for revenue only. Against this theory of tariff-making Clay opposed a system of high duties which would have the effect of encouraging the development of industry in the United States by protecting it against the competition of goods and manufactures of alien origin. The great Whig statesman's championship of a protective tariff dated from his term as Senator from Kentucky in 1809, but it was not until 1828 that his ideas prevailed in the enactment of a tariff whose excessive rates were opposed by John C. Calhoun and other prominent legislators, although Daniel Webster, who theretofore had been aligned against protective tariffs, supported the measure.

The act had been passed by the solid vote of the Middle States and those of the West, with divided support from the legislators of New England. It was denounced by the South as a "tariff of abominations," which took no account of economic considerations but was distinctly sectional, protecting manufacturers in one area of the country, while adversely affecting them in another. Vice President Calhoun voiced the disapproval by his state, South Carolina, of the act as inimical to its agricultural interests and issued the South Carolina Exposition, which caused the agitation of the question of State sovereignty and nullification and led to the great Hayne-Webster debate in the Senate in 1830.

The "tariff of abominations" was modified slightly in 1830, and in 1832 was superseded by the Act of 1832, but neither law satisfied the South.

"Half horse and half alligator."

(1820)

IN THE picturesque language of the early American border any especially tough character was termed "half horse and half alligator." The appellation was a favorite with the self-proclaimed bad men, the "screamers" and "ring-tailed roarers" of the American backwoods regions. "The Kentucky Hunters," they of the long rifles; Davy Crockett, frontiersman and politician; and Mike Fink, the fabulous dead-shot and his followers among the rakehell crews of the keel boats they poled down the Ohio and Lower Mississippi rivers, all announced whenever they had an appreciative audience that they were the authentic article, that they could lick their weight in wildcats.

The band of river pilots, horse thieves, and slave kidnapers who under the leadership of John A. Murrell terrorized the old Southwest during the first two decades of the nineteenth century were perhaps the most notorious bad men in the monster category. Murrell's outlaws, composed of local gangs whose personnel frequently changed, operated in eight States, attacking the flatboats that were poled down the Ohio and Mississippi Rivers, stealing horses, raiding towns and plantations, and carrying away slaves for ransom. So many and flagrant were their outrages that Murrell became a fearsome, almost legendary, figure.

He was born in middle Tennessee and began his career of crime early, at the age of twenty-two having been tried twice for horse stealing, for which he served a year in jail upon his conviction at his second trial. Upon his release he organized local gangs that committed highway robberies in states from Georgia to Louisiana, with special attention to the vicinity of New Orleans. After eight years of depredations by land and river, Murrell was captured in 1834 and convicted on a charge of Negro stealing. He served a sentence of ten years, and died soon after his release in 1844.

"The Almighty Dollar, that great object of universal de-
votion throughout our land."

Washington Irving (1783-1859)

To THE mildly critical attitude toward business of a kindly
man of scholarly tastes the language owes a phrase widely
used to characterize crass money-getting. Washington Irving's aside in his description of an idyllic little community,
which occurs in *The Creole Village*, published in 1837,
was the observation of a man then in his prime who had
seen the transition of the Republic from "the gristle to
the bone." The nation by that time had definitely veered
from the purely agricultural economy envisioned for it by
Jefferson and was adopting the industrial economy advocated by Hamilton.

Irving himself, by temperament unfitted to engage in
mere money-making, was disinclined to engage in business.
His interests were cultural; intellectual pursuits and the
pleasures of gracious living seemed to him far more worth
while than the amassing of wealth. Definitely, he was not
commercially minded, and the emphasis he saw placed on
the power of money that attended the country's industrial
development was foreign to his thought and sympathies.

But it was characteristic of Irving's genial, kindly philosophy that he did not engage in any diatribes against
this trend. Notwithstanding, his telling phrase has continued to be a favorite with those who inveigh against
undue materialism.

"Down With the Rent!"

(1840)

NEW YORK, the only State in the Union where a quasi-feudal system of land tenures prevailed, was the scene in the 1840's of an Anti-Rent War. Thousands of resentful tenants on great estates in a dozen counties of New York, occupied their farms on leaseholds which conferred only a nominal title limited by annual rental payments, some personal service, and numerous restrictions on the right of future resale.

The greatest of these vast land grants, which antedated the foundation of the Republic, covered the present counties of Albany and Rensselaer and part of Columbia, running for twenty-four miles along the Hudson and twenty-four miles inland on each side of the river.

The discontent of the leaseholders came to a head in 1840, after the death in January preceding of Stephen Van Rensselaer, "last of the patroons." He had been an indulgent landlord, so that at his death he left nearly $400,000 in uncollected and long-overdue rents. His heirs, not so indulgent, demanded payment. The majority of the tenants met in convention in July and pledged themselves to resist all "feudal exactions." When the sheriff of Albany county vainly attempted to serve warrants on the non-paying farmers three companies of state militia were required for his protection. The aroused farmers donned Indian war paint and feathers, and by means of blasts from tin horns warned the countryside whenever a sheriff's posse appeared. Their battle cry was "Down With the Rent!"

The situation became acute when one of their leaders was arrested in 1844 and put on trial for stopping the sheriff of Columbia county and seizing and burning his papers. The conviction of the leader brought to the farmers the realization that redress of their grievances must be accomplished by legal means.

In 1846, a new state constitution was ratified, and it contained clauses abolishing feudal tenures and limiting to a period of not more than twelve years any future agricultural lease in which any rent or service was reserved.

* * *

"What hath God wrought!"

Samuel Finley Breese Morse (1791-1872)

ALTHOUGH SUCCESSFUL as an artist, especially as a portrait painter, Samuel F. B. Morse, inventor of the electro-magnetic telegraph, abandoned the practice of art for the study of science. Prior to his supreme achievement in the latter field he had given much study to chemistry and, in particular, to electrical and galvanic experiments. He conceived the idea of a magnetic telegraph in 1832 while on a sea voyage, and for four years thereafter he worked on the idea. He completed a working model of an electromagnetic recording telegraph in 1836, which he demonstrated to the Congress the next year. He then went abroad and unsuccessfully sought to interest the governments of England and France in his invention.

Six years of efforts were rewarded when Congress in the closing moments of a midnight session in 1843 appropriated $30,000 for the construction of an experimental line between Washington and Baltimore. When the line was completed and the instruments installed, Morse from the Capitol in Washington on May 24, 1844, sent over the wires to Baltimore the historic words, "What hath God wrought!" The message was correctly repeated to him by Alfred Vail, his partner, in Baltimore, and the success of the magnetic telegraph was demonstrated.

"Sold down the river."

(*1850*)

APOLOGISTS FOR slavery contend that the picture of it given in *Uncle Tom's Cabin* was not typical. That there were grave faults and abuses inherent in it they do not deny, but they argue that, in the main, slave-holders, if for no other reason than that of self-interest, did not mistreat their human property.

Aside from occasional physical maltreatment of slaves, one of the most cruel features of the system was the traffic in them practiced by some owners. This involved the separation of families, with a callous disregard of the feelings and affections of the members thus separated. The humane slave-holders as a rule did not regard their slaves as properly objects of barter and sale for profit, but rather as a means of cheap labor, as household servants, and as essential in an agrarian economy. Most of the owners in this class felt an obligation to provide adequate shelter, food, clothing and health measures, and even recreation for their slaves.

This was especially true of slavery in the older Southern states, where generations of slaves were born and lived. They had a deep affection for the only land they knew and an attachment to masters who had treated them kindly. But as the cultivation of cotton became centered in the Deep South, the states bordering on the Mississippi river, the situation as to slavery there changed. Conditions there were far different from those prevailing in the older states, where the slaves regarded themselves as superior to those in bondage in the states where Cotton was King.

Consequently to be "sold down the river," separated from their native homes, and too often, from their families, was regarded as a tragic fate by slaves in the older communities.

The phrase has survived, with a modern meaning hardly different from the original. As used now, it implies an action taken summarily and without regard to the wishes of the person affected by it.

*   *   *

"Cotton is King."

David Christy (1802-1867?)

THERE WAS general agreement in the Deep South prior to the Civil War that its principal staple was indeed supreme in its agricultural economy. There was good reason for this opinion, for cotton was the wealth of that section.

The value of the crop had increased steadily, aided measurably by slave labor, and by 1850 it had reached a total of more than $100,000,000 annually. In that year cotton constituted about half of the total exports of the United States.

Cotton is King, or the Economical Relations of Slavery, was the title of a book by David Christy, published in 1855. Christy was an anti-slavery writer who advocated colonization of Negro slaves and was not wholly in sympathy with the methods of abolitionists. The object of his book, as he explained, was "to convince the abolitionists of the utter failure of their plans."

"A peculiar institution."

(*1854*)

EVEN BEFORE the adoption of the Constitution, slavery was regarded as an anomaly in the United States. It did not accord with the plain assertion in the Declaration of Independence "that all men are created equal," with the "unalienable rights" of "life, liberty and the pursuit of happiness." The framers of the Constitution had been careful to avoid making any mention of "slaves" or "slavery" in the document, and it contained no inhibition against the institution within the boundaries of the forming Republic. There were men among the Founding Fathers, notably Washington, Madison, Franklin, and Hamilton, who were opposed to slavery. And of the signers of the Declaration of Independence, John Adams and Thomas Jefferson, deplored the existence of slavery in this country, Jefferson saying of it: "I tremble for my country when I reflect that God is just."

The silence of the Constitution about a matter so important was in deference to the insistence of Southern states that there should be no interference with slavery, South Carolina making this a condition of its entrance into the Union. Opposition to slavery was strongest in the North, where industry was predominant over agriculture, and several States there either before or soon after the establishment of the Union abolished it or provided for its eventual abolition.

Slavery became known as an institution "peculiar" to the South, where climatic conditions and the purely agrarian character of its economy were favorable to it. Among the earliest known printed references to it as "a peculiar institution" was one in an article in the *New York Tribune* of October 19, 1854.

"Pike's Peak or Bust."

(1858)

WHEN GOLD was struck in the foothills of the Rockies near Pike's Peak, Colorado, in 1858, thousands of fortune-seeking Americans set forth for the new El Dorado. Coming after the depression of 1857, the discovery stirred hopes that the California gold strike of 1848 would be equalled or excelled.

Hordes of treasure seekers from regions east of the mountains crossed the plains in covered wagons, in carriages, on horseback, and even on foot pushing or drawing carts laden with their effects. In two years 35,000 gold seekers had gone to Colorado, and Denver, its principal city, boomed.

Of those lured by the prospects of riches, all were inspired by the rallying cry "Pike's Peak or Bust." Not all reached their destination, however, and many wagons were left along the trail. With characteristic American good humor some of them bore on their wagon flaps the painted legend, "Busted, By Gosh!"

"The Lord prefers common-looking people. That is the reason He makes so many of them."

Abraham Lincoln

INNUMERABLE ANECDOTES, as well as actual incidents, told of Abraham Lincoln attest his abiding interest in and concern for the masses of the people. His unassuming humility, which was a prominent trait and really served to accentuate his greatness, proceeded from a consciousness that he himself sprang from the common people. He was not given to preachment, but his complete lack of any sort of vanity in itself was an outspoken reproof of those who took pride in their birth, high station in life or the possession of personal qualities that, in their opinion, set them above the common run of their fellows.

Lincoln's often quoted phrase about the prevalence of the common man in the world occurred in his account of a dream he had. In this dream, he related, he was in a crowd, one of whom recognized him and in a surprised tone said: "He is a very common-looking man," to which Lincoln replied: "Friend, the Lord prefers common-looking people. That is why He makes so many of them."

This remark, characteristic of Lincoln's wit, so exactly accords with his well known sentiments that the dream could have been invented by him as a way both to show that he was conscious of his own physical homeliness and how little it mattered in the Divine scheme of things. It is known, however, that on several occasions he related dreams he had had and, although not superstitious, had even been disturbed by some of them. It seems possible, therefore, that he actually had had this particular dream.

"Where there is no vision, the people perish."
                    Ralph Waldo Emerson (1803-1882)

To THE materialist view of human life Ralph Waldo
Emerson ever opposed the philosophy of idealism. In the
United States of his times he saw many evidences that the
people, and among them even men of the learned profes-
sions and of superior educational advantages were actuated
in their strivings by their desire for material rewards rather
than by the good their labors might accomplish. He saw
in this a danger to what he called the art of thinking.

In his address before the literary societies of Waterville
College, in 1863, on *The Man of Letters,* he deprecated
this spirit and appealed to his listeners to aspire to higher
ideals. An accusation against this country, he said, was
that it alone among all the nations failed to balance labor
by mental activity, that as a people we were skeptical,
frivolous, narrow in our religious creeds, and lacked an
affirmative philosophy.

American life, he asserted, had become expensive, therefore greedy, and our eyes were turned earthward, not up-
ward to the sky. Quoting a "current oracle," that nations
die by suicide, a sign of which was the decay of thought,
he declared that "Where there is no vision, the people
perish."

"There is more law at the end of a policeman's nightstick than in a decision of the Supreme Court."

(1867)

NEW YORK CITY's submerged districts after the Civil War were infested by gangs of young toughs and petty thieves, forerunners of the more vicious organized bands of gunmen, bootleggers, and racketeers that flourished in American cities during the two decades following the First World War. The earlier gangsters were especially active in the "Gas House District," an area in the city's lower East Side, where they looted stores, preyed on the residents, harassed the police, and in general, terrorized law-abiding citizens in the district.

They constituted a serious police problem, which was partly solved by the forthright methods of the commander of the precinct, a robust police captain known as "Clubber" Williams. His remedy for conditions was an order to his men to break up the gangs by the vigorous wielding of their nightsticks upon lawbreakers. He did not hesitate himself to carry out his orders to his men and became one to be feared by the gangsters. Whether or not he originated the aphorism that "There is more law at the end of a policeman's nightstick than in a decision of the Supreme Court," it is certain that he applied the theory of nightstick law in his precinct.

"The Man in the Street."

Ralph Waldo Emerson

HENRY A. WALLACE'S "common man" had his prototype many years before he became the Vice President's special object of solicitude. As the unit of the most numerous element of a population, although not always its most powerful or influential, the "man in the street" is regarded as representing the thoughts and feelings of the multitude. Even before the expression occurred in Ralph Waldo Emerson's essay, Charles Fulke Greville, English diarist, used it in his *Memoirs,* published in 1830. To convey the thought that the masses usually are not unaware of the designs of government, Greville wrote: "knowing as the 'man in the street' . . . always does, the greatest secrets of kings . . ."

Emerson used the phrase in a somewhat different sense. "The man in the street does not know a star in the sky," he wrote in *The Conduct of Life: Worship,* published in 1866, the implication being that the average man is too engrossed in mundane affairs to realize the higher value and desirability of things spiritual.

Today orators, publicists and writers are fond of citing the "man in the street" as a common denominator, the repository of homely wisdom about politics, economics, and business, and as a force to be reckoned with by government, politicians, and business men.

"Forty Acres And a Mule."

(1866)

AT THE close of the Civil War conditions in the South were chaotic and the plight of thousands of Negroes suddenly freed became serious. Freedmen willing to work were unable to obtain employment from their former masters, now impoverished. Many others among the liberated slaves refused to work for wages, deluded by the promises of demagogues that Congress would divide the lands of the planters among their former slaves.

Many Negroes flocked to the army camps to be fed, and soldiers in joking mood encouraged them in their expectations that a benevolent government would provide every freedman with "Forty acres and a mule."

The expression became current as a derisive commentary on the extravagant hopes aroused among former slaves by the reconstructionist policies.

"Men, their rights and nothing more; women, their rights and nothing less."

Susan Brownell Anthony (1820-1906)

FROM THE organization of the woman suffrage movement in 1848 until the adoption of the Nineteenth Amendment of the Constitution in August 1920, a long span of years intervened during which many other social reforms were accomplished. Seventy-two years before, the first Woman Suffrage Convention was called in Seneca Falls, New York, by Elizabeth Cady Stanton, Lucretia Mott, and Susan B. Anthony.

Almost from her girlhood Miss Anthony had been wholeheartedly devoted to the cause of abolition of slavery, and the transition from that cause to the advocacy of freedom for women was easy. For years she spoke, wrote and worked to obtain full legal rights for women, heedless of ridicule and rebuffs, and confident in the ultimate success of the movement, of which she frequently said, "failure is impossible."

To obtain the publicity for the cause that her requests of editors were not always successful in getting, she started a newspaper, *Revolution,* in 1868. Its motto was "The true Republic—men, their rights and nothing more; women, their rights and nothing less."

When the Fourteenth Amendment to the Constitution was adopted she decided to test its guaranty of citizenship by casting a vote in the Presidential election of 1872, for which she was arrested and tried. She was found guilty and fined $100. She respectfully told the Court that she would never pay a dollar of the fine, and she never did. But the cause in which she had fought so valiantly was not won until fourteen years after her death.

"The way to resume is to resume."

John Sherman (1823-1900)

REHABILITATION OF the nation's finances was one of the nation's greatest problems at the close of the Civil War. "Greenbacks," known by the color of the ink in which they were engraved, had been used to finance a costly war, and had caused a great inflation of the currency. At the end of the war there were more than $400,000,000 of such money in circulation in the United States.

John Sherman, Senator from Ohio, as chairman of the Senate finance committee in 1867, took a leading part in the discussions relative to the matter of putting the nation's monetary system on a sound basis. During the war he had helped as a representative in the Congress to give greenbacks the status of legal tender, but he believed that eventually they must be retired and specie payments resumed.

"The way to resume is to resume," he declared, and he proposed a plan of funding greenbacks into government bonds. A Resumption Act was enacted in 1875, but the plan was not that advocated by Sherman but one by Senator George F. Edmunds of Vermont, which provided for the resumption of specie payment on January 1, 1879, and authorized the Secretary of the Treasury to accumulate a gold fund with which to redeem the greenbacks on demand.

Sherman, who was a younger brother of General William Tecumseh Sherman of Civil War fame, had early made finance his special field. After his service in the Senate he was Secretary of the Treasury from 1877 to 1881, and then returned to the Senate. He became Secretary of State under President McKinley, but resigned soon after this country declared war on Spain in 1898.

"The Robber Barons."

Matthew Josephson (1899-   )

IN MEDIEVAL times petty noblemen in central European countries established their castle strongholds at strategic points commanding main-traveled roads and exacted tribute from all wayfarers for safe conduct through the territory over which they ruled. A rough analogy between these "robber barons" and the commanding figures in American industry in the period between the close of the Civil War and the turn of the century was drawn by Matthew Josephson in his book of that title. He saw in the bold and somewhat ruthless but amplified and refined, methods of these American industrialists a similarity to those employed by the predatory nobles of the Middle Ages who had enriched themselves at the expense of others who were in their power.

Some of the more prominent among the founders of great American fortunes singled out by Josephson as the "robber barons" were the Rockefellers, Henry M. Flagler, John D. Archbold, Oliver H. Payne, H. H. Rogers and others, of the Standard Oil Trust; the Morgans and Jay Cooke in banking and finance; the Vanderbilts, Jay Gould, James J. Fisk, Daniel Drew, Collis P. Huntington, Leland Stanford, James J. Hill and Edward H. Harriman in railroading; Andrew Carnegie, Henry C. Frick and Charles M. Schwab in steel; the Armours in beef; John Jacob Astor, in furs; and H. D. Havemeyer, in sugar.

"The Dollar of Our Daddies."

(1873)

AGITATION FOR the free coinage of silver, which was to continue through the last quarter of the century, became acute in 1873. In that year a revision of the coinage laws of the United States resulted in the withdrawal from circulation of the silver dollar, the country went on the gold standard, with paper currency and small silver coins circulating for convenience. This "Crime of '73" was considered by the farmers and silver miners of the West to be the cause of all their economic ills and they demanded the restoration to circulation of "The Dollar of Our Daddies," the allusion being to the coinage under the bimetallic basis which had been legally established in 1837 and prevailed until the Civil War.

Their agitation was resultful in bringing about the passage by the Congress in 1878 of the Bland-Allison Act which restored to circulation the silver dollar of 1837, making it full legal tender except where contracts specified payments to be made otherwise. The Treasury was required to purchase monthly not less than two million dollars' worth of silver bullion, nor more than four million dollars' worth, for coinage. In 1893 the policy of purchasing silver was discontinued.

"Let no guilty man escape."

Ulysses Simpson Grant

A MAJOR scandal in Grant's second administration was the exposure in 1875 of the Whiskey Ring, a secret association of distillers and Federal officials by which the government was defrauded of millions of dollars. The frauds were discovered principally through the efforts of the Secretary of the Treasury, Benjamin H. Bristow, and sixteen distilleries were seized and some 240 indictments were returned against distillers and Federal officials.

Although the President himself was guiltless of any connection with the frauds, the scandal reached to his official family, for one of the men indicted was O. E. Babcock, Grant's private secretary and confidential adviser.

The President's words, quoted in the foregoing were his indorsement on a letter of Bristow's containing the charges against Babcock which, with corroborating evidence, was laid before Grant July 29, 1875. To the order the President added: "No personal consideration should stand in the way of performing a public duty."

"The Chinese Must Go."

Denis Kearney (1847-1907)

The depression of 1877 was especially severe in San Francisco. The slump in business had the usual accompaniment of unemployment, and this was aggravated by the competition of cheap coolie labor. Thousands of Chinese laborers had been imported into California and there was great public resentment against the immigration of Asiatics to Pacific Coast States.

As unemployment increased, this feeling was intensified, finding its most inflammatory expression in the agitation by Denis Kearney. Kearney was a drayman with little formal education but with considerable powers of leadership, and his radical utterances were effective in stirring up a mob spirit in the city.

He denounced Chinese cheap labor, the dominance of capitalists, and business and commercial interests, especially the Central Pacific Railroad, which he held to be chiefly responsible for Chinese immigration, the central theme of his harangues being "The Chinese must go!"

His following grew and he organized the Workingmen's Party of California which spread throughout the state and for a time gave promise of becoming a political party of real power and influence.

"The Four Hundred."

Ward McAllister (1827-1895)

THE SWOLLEN fortunes that marked the years succeeding the close of the Civil War in the United States begot a class of people who were ambitious to be accepted as members of the most select society in the various large cities of the country, especially New York. From time to time self-constituted arbiters attempted to dictate who among the newly-rich should be considered eligible to membership in Society's inner circle. Among the earliest and most successful of these judges of social acceptability was Ward McAllister, Southern-born and himself a leader in New York Society.

When the matter of invitations to the Centennial ball, New York's premier annual social event, came up in 1876, McAllister counseled discrimination based on his estimate that the smart set of the city consisted of only four hundred persons.

Although many historians of New York Society held that the number actually was six hundred, McAllister's arbitrary delimitation has persisted as a ready term to denote coteries of the socially elect.

"The tariff question is a local question."
Winfield Scott Hancock (1824-1886)

FOR MANY years it was the practice in Presidential campaigns, when it might happen that there were no major issues, to invoke the tariff question. In the campaign of 1880 there were no outstanding points of difference on national questions between the Republican and Democratic parties, but as always they could fall back on the tariff differences.

General Winfield Scott Hancock, of Pennsylvania, was the candidate of the Democratic party for President that year, running against James A. Garfield, of Ohio, the Republican nominee. Hancock had received a large number of votes in 1868 for the Democratic nomination, but he was inexperienced in politics, possessed little knowledge of the problems of government. He was, however, a veteran of both the Mexican and Civil Wars and had a distinguished military record as a commander in the Union Army. It was on this record that he had been chosen by the Democrats.

The campaign of 1880 and, unfortunately, Hancock himself as a political figure, are remembered chiefly for a remark of the Democratic candidate which at the time caused widespread amused comment. In the course of an interview published in the Paterson (New Jersey) *Daily Guardian* of October 8, 1880, Hancock was quoted as saying:

"The tariff is a local question."

The reaction of the press of the country to the naive statement was one of ridicule and derision. More recent comment in some instances has been kinder, for it has been pointed out that a tariff bill usually is the sum of sectional, or local, demands which, at times, do not take into account the interests of the nation as a whole.

"The public be damned."

William Henry Vanderbilt (1821-1885)

METHODS OF railroad financing in the United States were in public disfavor in the Seventies and discontent was greatly increased by the report in 1879 of A. Barton Hepburn, of New York, on railroad freight rate discrimination.

It was at about the time of publication of the Hepburn report that William H. Vanderbilt, president of the New York Central System in a moment of anger uttered the words which came to be regarded as typifying the attitude of important financiers toward the public.

As related by Melville E. Stone in *Fifty Years A Journalist,* Vanderbilt had arrived in Chicago in his private car which was sidetracked in the yards of the Michigan Central Railroad. As he was at dinner with some friends a free-lance reporter entered the car unannounced and requested an interview with Vanderbilt, who asked him to wait until he had finished his dinner. The reporter, however was insistent, protesting that it was late, that he would not be able to return to his office in time to have the interview printed, that "the public—"

At this point Vanderbilt was out of patience and angrily interrupted:

"The public be damned; you get out of here."

The published newspaper version of the interview caused much adverse criticism and served to increase the prevailing unfriendliness of the public. A year later Vanderbilt, then in failing health, resigned all of his railroad presidencies.

"The dirty little coward that shot Mr. Howard."

(1882)

JESSE JAMES and his elder brother Frank had been members of Quantrell's guerillas who fought and raided and pillaged under the guise of Confederate soldiers in the Civil War and who were despised by Confederate and Union soldiers alike. Their service with Quantrell was good training for the James boys and for years the gang lived off the plunder of banks and railroads mainly. Partly because of the terror they inspired, and also because of the sympathies of their neighbors in western Missouri, many of whom were former adherents of the Confederacy, the outlaws escaped capture, and between raids went more or less openly.

As the depredations of the gang became ever more outrageous the Governor of Missouri offered a reward of $10,000 for the body of Jesse James, dead or alive.

The offer was too tempting to be resisted by at least two men. Their opportunity came when early in November 1881 Jesse, his wife and two children went to St. Joseph, Missouri, where under the name of Howard he rented a house. Two members of his gang, Robert and Charles Ford, lived with the family. On the morning of April 2, 1882, a warm day, Jesse unstrapped the belt holding the two revolvers he always carried and laid them down. As he mounted a chair to dust some pictures on the wall, they silently moved to a position between Jesse and his weapons. Both brothers drew their revolvers, but only Robert fired. The bullet struck Jesse at the base of the skull, and he died soon after in the arms of his wife. The line in the chorus of *The Ballad of Jesse James*, " . . . that dirty little coward that shot Mister Howard," reflected the feeling of many people, even those who condemned the outlaw chief's crimes, but abhorred the treachery by which his death was accomplished.

"The Strenuous Life."

Theodore Roosevelt

WHEN THE United States emerged from the Spanish-American War in 1898 a world power, Theodore Roosevelt, who had taken a picturesque if not decisive part in that struggle, saw a new destiny unfolding for the nation. His own dynamic personality, first made known generally by his record in the war, henceforth was to be frequently dramatized by his words and actions and to make him a legend.

His address before the Hamilton Club in Chicago in April 1899, in which he declared: "I wish to preach, not the doctrine of ignoble ease, but the doctrine of the strenuous life," was to further identify him in the public mind as a devotee of vigorous, if not violent, physical effort.

Roosevelt was that, of course, but the whole tenor of his Chicago address was directed to arousing Americans to a sense of their civic duties and the demands and responsibilities of their citizenship. The country called upon them, he declared, for "strenuous endeavor, not a life of ease." The reasoned, temperate words of this appeal later were to be exchanged for his vigorously expressed denunciations of "mollycoddles," "milksops," and "sissies."

"Without due process of law."

Fourteenth Amendment,
United States Constitution

LINCOLN'S EMANCIPATION of the slaves, while it gave them
freedom, did not make them citizens of the United States
or give them the franchise. It remained for the Fourteenth
Amendment to the Constitution, adopted in July 1868, to
accomplish this. The Thirteenth Amendment, adopted in
December 1865, had formally abolished slavery but contained no provision for giving the franchise to the emancipated slaves.

The first section of the Fourteenth Amendment, which
specifically conferred citizenship, provides that: "All persons born or naturalized in the United States, and subject
to the jurisdiction thereof, are citizens of the United
States and of the State wherein they reside." The section
furthermore guarantees such citizens against the enactment or enforcing of any State law "which shall abridge
the privileges and immunities" of citizens; "nor shall any
State deprive any person of life, liberty, or property, without due process of law. . . ."

When this amendment was adopted it was generally understood to have been designed to protect the newly
emancipated slaves in the enjoyment of civil rights, a guaranty further strengthened by the adoption two years
later of the Fifteenth Amendment, which declares that
"the right of citizens of the United States to vote shall not
be denied or abridged by the United States or any state
on account of race, color, or previous condition of serv-
itude."

As American industry in the post-war years developed
and State legislatures passed regulatory laws considered
by corporations to be repressive, a new interpretation of
the Fourteenth Amendment was made by the Supreme
Court of the United States to which suits were appealed

from State court decisions by corporation lawyers. By this interpretation corporations were held to be "persons" at law and therefore protected by the amendment from being deprived of their property "without due process of law." As early as 1886 the high Court decided that the amendment was not limited to the protection of citizens, but included corporations as well. In 1889 the Court decided that, while State authorities could regulate railroad rates, they could not fix such rates so low as to deprive the companies of their properties "without due process of law," but must allow them a reasonable profit.

Before the end of the nineteenth century a great many decisions of the Supreme Court had pretty well established as a principle of law, under the re-interpretation of this amendment, that it guaranteed liberty, not only as a civil right, but also as a property right.

The phrase "without due process of law" occurs also in the Fifth Amendment, in the Bill of Rights, by which citizens are protected against double jeopardy, self-incrimination, and deprivation of life, liberty or property without due process of law. But as the Fourteenth Amendment has been construed as holding that corporations are "persons," it is that amendment which is invoked by corporations seeking relief against State laws which they consider to be confiscatory of their property or otherwise unduly oppressive.

"How the other half lives."

Jacob August Riis (1840-1914)

THE POWER of words was well demonstrated in the case of Jacob A. Riis' book, *How the Other Half Lives.* The book, written in 1890, was a factual account of conditions in New York City's tenement houses, the dirt, disease, poverty and degradation of the dwellers, and the responsibility of society for a betterment of their situation.

After reading it, Theodore Roosevelt, then Police Commissioner of New York City, called at Riis' office in the heart of the slum district. As Riis was absent at the time, Roosevelt left his card on which he wrote, "I have read your book and have come to help."

And he did help. He and Riis became life-long friends and together they labored to erase the vile conditions which Riis had described both in his writing as a newspaper reporter and in his book. Through his efforts and those of Roosevelt a Tenement House Commission was created, the notorious tenement district known as Mulberry Bend was cleared and eventually became a park, and living conditions generally among the very poor of the district were bettered.

Riis was a Danish emigrant of good family who came to this country in 1870. He had worked as a carpenter, coal miner, farm laborer, traveling salesman and newspaper man, and knew at first hand the seamy side of life. But it was as a police reporter, one who was more interested in the causes and prevention of crime than in crime itself, that his compassion was aroused and his efforts exerted.

"The mother of trusts."

Henry Osborne Havemeyer (*1847-1907*)

WHILE THE Standard Oil Trust, formed in 1882 by John D. Rockefeller and his associates, is commonly thought of as "the mother of trusts," because it was the first in the field and the model for later comers, it was H. O. Havemeyer, organizer of the Sugar Trust, who first ascribed the maternity of trusts to a quite different source.

Havemeyer, who in 1891, formed the American Sugar Refining Company with a virtual monopoly of sugar in this country, declared that the protective tariff was the mother of trusts.

In the sense that the Standard Oil Trust provided the model for many successor companies, however, it can fairly be considered the originator of this form of business organization. As originally formed, it consisted of the deposit of some forty companies engaged in the several branches of the oil industry, of their shares in trust to nine trustees. The stockholders received in exchange trust certificates of a face value of $100, and the trustees controlled two-thirds of all the shares, became stockholders of all the companies in the combination with power to serve as directors in each of them and to be in full control of all the properties of the constituent companies of the trust.

"Kansas has started in to raise hell, and she seems to have an overproduction."

William Allen White

THE MCKINLEY-BRYAN presidential campaign of 1896, coming close upon the demise of the Populist Party which had its stamping-ground in Kansas, found many people receptive to the doctrines of economic reform advocated in the Democratic platform. Kansas farmers were severely hit by the depression, low prices, and the high rate of interest on farm mortgages which had caused numerous foreclosures. This condition had been favorable to the prevalence of agitators and radical speakers who found ready listeners in Kansas. Prominent among the radicals was Mary Ellen Lease who aroused the enthusiasm of her hearers by telling them that they should "raise more hell and less corn."

William Allen White, the young editor of the Emporia *Gazette,* was among the most ardent upholders of the established order. This was at a period in his life antecedent to his adoption of the liberal principles for which he became noted. At the height of the 1896 campaign, on August 15, he was heckled and jeered on the street in Emporia.

Returning to his office, White wrote the editorial, "What's The Matter With Kansas?" which appeared in that evening's issue of the *Gazette.* The wit and ardor of the editorial, which was widely reprinted and quoted, attracted nation-wide attention. The closing sentences of the editorial by which it is best remembered were: "What's the matter with Kansas? Nothing under the shining sun. She is losing wealth, population and standing. She has got her statesmen, and the money power is afraid of her. Kansas is all right. She has started in to raise hell, as Mrs. Lease advised, and she seems to have an overproduction."

"Certain malefactors of great wealth."

Theodore Roosevelt

FINANCIAL INTERESTS at feud with the administration of
President Theodore Roosevelt blamed him for the stock
market panic of 1907. The President had consistently advocated the regulation of the railroads and supervision of
their rates by the government and a bill incorporating his
ideas was introduced in the House January 4, 1906, by
Representative Peter Hepburn of Iowa, and after a bitter
debate in the Senate it was passed March 18, 1906.

Wall Street's reaction to the measure was one of fear
and apprehension. Railroad stocks declined, and the
prices of industrial shares reflected the uneasiness of the
railroads. By 1907, the stock market panic had set in, and
the President was accused by the great financial interests
of having brought it on by undermining public confidence
in railroad securities.

Roosevelt, asserting that he was not opposed to wealth
itself but only to those who abused the power of wealth,
held that speculation by big financiers was really responsible for the troubles of the stock market. In a speech at
Provincetown, Massachusetts, on August 20, 1907, he declared that "certain malefactors of great wealth," whom
he did not name, might have banded together "to bring
about as much financial stress as possible."

"Corrupt and Contented."

Joseph Lincoln Steffens (1866-1936)

AMERICAN MUNICIPALITIES, especially those of metropolitan status, were boss-ridden and misgoverned in the early years of this century. Graft, misuse of public funds, crooked deals, stolen elections, and corrupt alliances between officials and criminal elements flourished and were common knowledge. Yet, except for a comparatively few civic reformers, the public was apathetic.

This notorious state of affairs gave the so-called "muckraking" writers their chance. Prominent in this class was Lincoln Steffens who, in 1903, became the managing editor of *McClure's Magazine,* a successful publication in New York City. Steffens, university trained, had been a police reporter on New York newspapers and had seen at first hand the squalor and misery of the city's slum dwellers, the working agreement between the police and criminals, and all the evils of a machine-controlled municipal government. He had a free hand in the editorial conduct of *McClure's* and resolved to make the magazine the organ of reformist expose writers.

Steffens himself investigated conditions in the most flagrant examples of corrupt city administrations and wrote the articles depicting these conditions. In succession, his accounts described the existing official crookedness in the boss-controlled cities of St. Louis, Minneapolis, Pittsburgh, Philadelphia, Chicago, and New York, and these articles subsequently were incorporated in a book, *The Shame of the Cities."*

It was difficult to single out any one of these cities as the worst example of municipal corruption, for in all of them a common pattern was followed. For his series of three articles on Philadelphia, however, Steffens' title, "Philadelphia: Corrupt and Contented," characterized the prevailing apathy of American city dwellers toward the

"steals and jobs," the election frauds by which crooks were
perpetuated in office, and the machine politics responsible
for such a condition.

*   *   *

"Men with the muckrake."

Theodore Roosevelt

"Muckrakers" owed its addition to the American vocabu-
lary to a sentence in a speech delivered by President
Theodore Roosevelt at the corner-stone laying of the
House office building in Washington on April 14, 1906.
Roosevelt's passion for reform had been the inspiration
for a "literature of exposure" of political and business and
financial evils, published in magazines in the first part
of the century.

He had not denounced any of the many articles of this
character, but the publication of David Graham Phillips'
series of articles, "The Treason of the Senate," incensed
Roosevelt.

"Men with the muck-rake are often indispensable to the
well-being of society", he declared in his address, "but
only if they know when to stop raking the muck."

"Dementia Americana: the unwritten law."

Delphin Michael Delmas (1844-1928)

ESCAPADES OF playboys and spenders, sons of wealthy parents, were many and notorious during the early part of this century. Harry Kendall Thaw, profligate son of a Pittsburgh millionaire was a central figure in many a madcap performance on New York City's "White Way." He had married Evelyn Nesbit, a beautiful show girl, but matrimony did not seem to have tamed him. He provided one of the greatest sensations the country's press ever recorded when, during a performance on the roof of Madison Square Garden, New York, he shot and killed Stanford White, member of a firm of architects who had designed some of the most noted structures in the country.

Thaw's trial on an indictment for murder in the first degree opened on June 22, 1907. His plea was justifiable homicide in defending his wife's honor against White. Testimony at the trial was all that the most avid seeker after the sensational could desire.

Thaw's lawyer, Delphin M. Delmas, "silver-tongued spell-binder of the Pacific Coast," in his speech to the jury gave to the language two word-coinages that have endured. He declared that Thaw in killing White had "struck for the purity of the wives and homes of America", that the mental furor caused by his discovery of White's conduct was a "brain-storm," and, probably having in mind Plato's definition of "unwritten law" as "that which has arisen from custom," he justified his client's act as one dictated by "dementia Americana; the unwritten law." District Attorney Jerome derided "brain-storm" as the "paranoia of the millionaire," and moved that a commission be appointed to pass on Thaw's sanity. Thaw was pronounced sane but the jury was unable to agree and was discharged after the trial had been in progress more than two months.

At his second trial in January 1908 the jury returned a verdict, "Not guilty because insane", and Thaw was committed to a State institution.

*   *   *

"Don't sell America short."

John Pierpont Morgan (1837-1913)

FAITH IN the destiny of the United States, in the Nation's ability to weather the severest financial and political storms and to emerge triumphant was an article in the business credo of J. Pierpont Morgan the Elder. Although temperamentally conservative, his financial operations were always on so huge a scale that they reflected his native optimism, which was a characteristic well known to other financiers.

Morgan had been a foremost figure in the financial world for many years and he had been especially active and effective in devising measures of relief in the money panic of 1907, and his coolness was an inspiration for men less stout-hearted than he.

The aphorism, "Don't be a bear on the United States", was a favorite with Morgan which has often been attributed to his father, Junius Spenser Morgan. In the public mind the revised version is the one associated with J. Pierpont Morgan.

"America is God's Melting-Pot."

Israel Zangwill (1864-1926)

IN A striking phrase that has lived, an Englishman characterized the process of fusing men and women of many divers races and nationalities into the amalgam of Americanism. Observing how the peoples of the Old World when living in the freer environment of the New, shed their inherited prejudices, antagonisms and the inhibitions bred into them by centuries of oppression and denial of human liberties, Israel Zangwill gave a drama form to his discussion of the subject.

"The Melting-Pot" was the title of his play which was produced in New York City in October 1908. The central theme of the play is expressed in the line in Act I:

"America is God's Melting-Pot where all the races of Europe are melting and re-forming."

Zangwill was born in London of Jewish parents. The subject of his many books was mainly the condition of the Jewish people in modern times. He had visited this country and studied the process of Americanization.

."I stand for the square deal."

Theodore Roosevelt

THEODORE ROOSEVELT's dissatisfaction with the administration of his successor in office was unconcealed by the
time President Taft had completed less than half of his
term. The relations between the former President and his
one-time friend and protege were strained, and a considerable element in the Republican party who were not in
sympathy with Taft policies looked to Roosevelt as their
leader. Although the Progressive Party had not yet been
born, the basic program of the party was to be foreshadowed by the man who was to be its leader.

Roosevelt early in August 1910, started on a tour of
the Middle West and West with his announced objective
Cheyenne, Wyoming, where he was to make an address
on the occasion of the celebration of Frontier Day on
August 27. He made speeches in several cities on the way
to Cheyenne and on his journey back East. It was at
Osawatomie, Kansas, on August 30 he made the significant
statement that caused much discussion throughout the
nation.

"I stand for the square deal," he declared, adding: "not
merely for fair play, under the present rules of the game,
but . . . for having these rules changed . . . for a more
substantial equality of opportunity and reward."

This was the first time he had publicly used the gambling term which became famous and which he probably
acquired during his experience as a cowboy. In a speech
delivered at the Minnesota State Fair on September 2,
1901, he said: "A man who is good enough to shed his
blood for his country is good enough to be given a square
deal afterward."

"Out Where the West Begins."

Arthur Chapman (1873-1935)

SECTIONAL PRIDE is a characteristic of American communities, finding its expression in various ways and on frequent occasions. Usually its most ardent promoters are the Chambers of Commerce and the civic associations of "booster" nature which are active in every American town and city. They are responsible for the picturesque appellations given to communities, descriptive of distinguishing features claimed for them.

This sectional spirit has been responsible also for considerable rivalry in which extraordinary qualities are attributed to communities by their respective champions. Arthur Chapman's poem, *Out Where the West Begins,* is one of the best known examples of a sectional pride that is expressed in lyrical terms. His verses emphasize qualities of persons, rather than physical or commercial advantages, as marking the West in contradistinction to the East. For

> *Out where the handclasp's a little stronger,*
> *Out where the smile dwells a little longer,*
> *That's where the West begins.**

Of course, the poem itemizes other virtues possessed by the people and section it lauds and they are all cited as the hall-mark of the West.

---

* From Arthur Chapman's *"Out Where the West Begins, and Other Western Verses,"* Houghton & Mifflin Co.

"The Seven Sisters."

(1913)

DISSOLUTION BY the courts of the Standard Oil Trust in 1890 was followed by the enactment of the Sherman Anti-Trust Law. When this act proved ineffective to halt the organization of great monopolistic combinations many states passed anti-trust laws. The laws of New Jersey long were noted, not only for their tolerance of monopolistic corporations, but also for the inducements they offered for their incorporation in that state, and many New York trusts had availed themselves of the encouragement offered them.

In the closing session of the New Jersey legislature of 1913, Woodrow Wilson, then Governor of the state, put through seven measures designed to curb trusts. These laws, popularly known as "The Seven Sisters," were patterned after the corporation statutes of California and were considered so drastic that many large corporations surrendered their New Jersey charters and re-incorporated under the more liberal laws of Delaware.

"The lunatic fringe."

Theodore Roosevelt

HIMSELF FOREMOST among public men of his generation
who sought the correction of evils in government and
business, Theodore Roosevelt did not hesitate to denounce
what he considered excesses of zeal or errors of judgment
of reformers. When the fervor of reformers reached its
boiling point in the "expose" articles that filled the columns of magazines during his administrations, he lashed
out at one of the writers as a "muck-raker," borrowing
the phrase from John Bunyan's *The Pilgrim's Progress*
to popularize his characterization.

Even after he had retired to private life and reviewed
his eventful career, the recollection of his experience with
men whose reformist activities ran counter to his views
moved him to vigorous expression.

". . . among the wise and high-minded people who in
self-respecting and genuine fashion strive earnestly for
peace," he wrote, "there are the foolish fanatics always to
be found in such a movement and always discrediting it—
the men who form the lunatic fringe in all reform movements."

"Pie in the Sky."

(1917)

JUST PRIOR tO the entrance of the United States into World War I the Industrial Workers of the World became active, especially in the lumber and mining regions of the Pacific States and in the West generally. This body, organized in 1906, was revolutionary in character and somewhat similar to the Syndicalists. Its radical nature is indicated by its adoption of the principle that "the working class and the employing class have nothing in common," that the struggle must go on, to the end that the control of the machinery of production must pass to the workers. Abolition of the wage system, class war, and the formation of "one big union" for all labor were objectives of the organization, which indorsed the Bolshevik regime in Russia.

The extreme radicalism of the I.W.W. found no favor with American organized labor generally, and its membership was made up largely of agitators, drifters, and wandering artisans. So numerous was this element that the organization was dubbed the "I Won't Work," and its members "Wobblies." The theme song adopted for the organization was "Pie in the Sky," a set of doggerel verses originally a hobo song, the burden of which was that work and prayer would be rewarded after death by "pie in the sky," instead of the hay upon which they had subsisted in life. The refrain added in the I.W.W. adaptation of the song was, "It's a lie," indicating the religious unbelief of its members.

Demonstrations by the organization during the war were so subversive of law and order, obstructive of the nation's war effort and so frequently accompanied by riots and violence that the Government resorted to repressive measures against it, and it virtually has ceased to exist.

"History is more or less bunk."

Henry Ford (1863-   )

BECAUSE OF an editorial attack on him by the Chicago *Tribune,* Henry Ford in 1919 sued the newspaper for libel, asking one million dollars damages. The libel alleged was based on an editorial titled "Ford Is An Anarchist," charging that the automobile manufacturer discriminated against workmen in his plant who had responded to a call to serve in the militia in the punitive expedition against Mexico just prior to the outbreak of World War I.

The trial of the suit was held in Mount Clemens, Michigan, and lasted from May until the middle of August, following. Ford was on the witness stand for more than a week, and the efforts of his cross-examination were to test his Americanism and to prove him illiterate. When he was asked to tell the jury "who was Benedict Arnold," he answered that Arnold was a writer. His error was due, his apologists have explained, to a momentary confusion of thought, Ford having in mind the writer, Arnold Bennett. It was following this answer that he remarked that "History is bunk." The remark was a reiteration of an opinion attributed to him in a newspaper interview in May 1916, when he was quoted as saying: "Records of old wars mean nothing to me. History is more or less bunk. It's tradition."

"The large mollycoddle vote."

Theodore Roosevelt

ANYTHING SAVORING of pacificism was anathema to Theo-dore Roosevelt. While professing himself to be a lover of peace—with some notable acts of his justifying the claim—his was not a docile or appeasing nature. As Assist-ant Secretary of the Navy he had worked earnestly to build up our sea armament. He had had a brief military career in the Spanish-American War as lieutenant colonel of the volunteer Rough Riders. As President he had sent the fleet around the world with the twofold purpose of dramatizing to the Nation the desirability of a strong Navy and as notice to Japan that this country was not to be intimidated. He had sped the completion of the Pan-ama Canal as necessary for the national defense and had insisted upon its fortification.

Out of office, as a private citizen he spoke and wrote for the military preparedness of the United States, and when it became apparent that this country inevitably would be drawn into the First World War his insistence upon measures of preparedness became ever more emphatic.

In his *Autobiography,* reviewing his efforts in this cause both before and after he became President, he re-ferred to "The large mollycoddle vote, people who are soft physically and morally." It was they, he wrote, who opposed preparedness, who voted against the building of battleships and the fortification of the canal, and their mistaken course was due to their pacifist character.

"They hired the money, didn't they?"

Calvin Coolidge

AT THE end of World War I the United States was the greatest creditor nation in the world. Our resources of men and treasure and the products of our industry had been made available without stint to the nations at war with Germany. Never in history had such vast sums of money and credit been advanced by a single nation to so many other countries. While the war lasted, no question was raised in any country as to the purely credit nature of this money. Not long after its close, however, there was agitation in France and Great Britain for either a scaling down of the amounts of the war debts or for their outright cancellation.

France on various grounds refused to make any payments whatever on the debts, while England paid annual instalments which subsequently dwindled down into token payments and eventually ceased altogether. The British had proposed to this country that payments by the debtor nations be conditioned on reparation payments by Germany, and when this country declined to accede to this suggestion there were sneers in the British press about "Uncle Shylock" and the pound of flesh.

President Calvin Coolidge was emphatically opposed to cancellation and made his position clear when, in his first message to the Congress in 1925, he declared: "I am opposed to cancellation of the foreign debts to America. These should be "paid as fast as possible," he added. Unofficially, and in characteristic New England locution, he expressed the homely opinion that borrowed money, even when owing to a nation by another nation, should be repaid.

"They hired the money, didn't they?" he asked. "Let them pay it."

"Rugged individualism."

Herbert Clark Hoover

WHILE THIS phrase, so often used derisively, is generally attributed to Hoover, he has disclaimed originating it. It had been used, he wrote, by American leaders for more than half a century before he used it. As employed by him, it appeared in a campaign speech delivered in New York on October 22, 1828, when he said:

"We were challenged with a peace-time choice between the American system of rugged individualism and a European philosophy of diametrically opposed doctrines—doctrines of paternalism and state socialism."

*   *   *

"Came the Dawn."

(1928)

WHEN THE sound track for motion pictures was perfected in 1929, the silent films were superseded by the "talkies" and with them came the dawn of the motion picture as an authentic drama form. Popular as the silent films were, they were not the serious contenders with the "legitimate stage" for public favor that the "talkies" proved to be. Necessarily those viewing the silent motion picture drama had to depend for their understanding of the story upon pantomime and also upon the explanatory titles flashed upon the screen at intervals.

How successful this pantomime could be was measured by the skill of the actors. The part played by titles was more simple, but the efforts of writers to give the literary touch to titles very often resulted in stilted phrases, and sometimes in bathos.

"Came the dawn," a favorite title to express the end of an anguished night of waiting, was adopted by critics of motion pictures as a symbol of pretentious title writing, as well as of the shortcomings of motion picture drama itself.

"A noble experiment."

Herbert Clark Hoover

WHAT PRESIDENT HOOVER really said of national prohibition was that it was "a great social and economic experiment, noble in motive and far-reaching in purpose."

This appraisal of an unpopular law was given in a letter of February 28, 1928, to Senator William E. Borah, of Idaho. Hoover repeated it, in his speech on August 11, 1928, accepting the Republican nomination for President. On that occasion he said, "I do not favor the repeal of the Eighteenth Amendment. I stand for the efficient enforcement of the laws enacted thereunder. . . . Our country has deliberately undertaken a great social and economic experiment, noble in motive, far-reaching in purpose."

Whatever the difference in meaning between this and the popular misquotation, the latter probably owes its currency to the uses of irony by the foes of prohibition.

* * *

"Prosperity is just around the corner."

(1932)

WHEN THE stock market crash of late 1929 was succeeded by a business depression that steadily worsened as industrial plants closed down and thousands of men and women were made idle, gloom settled over the country generally. Bankers, economists, business leaders, and spokesmen of the national government through the written and the spoken word vainly sought to dispel the prevailing pessimism and to reassure the public as to the nation's future. Their repeated assurances that basically the country's economy was sound and that the return of normal conditions was imminent were condensed into the popular phrase, "Prosperity is just around the corner." But as the depression continued and became intensified, the phrase came to be used derisively.

"The Era of Wonderful Nonsense."

Westbrook Pegler (1894-   )

PERHAPS NO single phrase so aptly characterized the Big Boom that ended in the stock market crash of 1929 as Westbrook Pegler's, "The Era of Wonderful Nonsense." In the phrase he epitomized the orgy of speculation, the extravagances of spending by those made newly rich, the · fabulous paper profits made in the stock market, and, in general, the frenzies of the bubble prosperity that marked the period of President Coolidge's administration.

Pegler, whose column "Fair Enough" was widely syndicated for newspaper publication, was an ironist and a merciless and unrestrained commentator on persons and happenings in the contemporary world. He first used the phrase in an article describing in his usual vein the spending antics of a comic artist made rich by the popularity of his drawings of a family created by his pen. The article later was included, under the title "Mr. Gump Himself," in a collection in Pegler's book *'Tain't Right*. Pegler himself recognized the aptness of his coinage of "The Era of Wonderful Nonsense," and used it frequently in subsequent articles.

"Taken for a ride."

(1930)

USUALLY THIEVES' jargon is unintelligible to any but themselves and to members of law-enforcing agencies. Only occasionally some slang phrase current in the underworld carries in itself any meaning to persons outside that world. "Taken for a ride," current during a gang-ridden period, is one of these.

A grimly descriptive phrase, it wrote finis to the closing chapter in the criminal career of many a gangster in the bootlegging and racketeer days that reached a climax in the nineteen thirties. In the great gangster centers of New York and Chicago the outlaws, while united in a common purpose to prey upon law-abiding communities, were divided into particular bands, each with its own leader, its recognized field of operations and its specialty in crime. As long as honor among thieves prevailed, peace existed between the several gangs. Encroachments upon territories or operations, however, were frequent, and inevitably gang feuds resulted.

When death was decreed by a gang leader, either for the member of a rival band or for some recalcitrant of his own, a favorite method was to take the doomed man "for a ride." That is, he was either lured or forced into an automobile containing his executioners. At some remote spot he was killed and his body tossed into some vacant lot or otherwise concealed. If it was desirable, for some reason, that the victim's fate be not known, his body was either destroyed or otherwise disposed of. One ghastly method of concealing the crime was to incase the body in cement and cast the solid mass into a lake or river.

"Brother, can you spare a dime?"

(1932)

As THE depression precipitated by the stock market crash of 1929 deepened and lengthened into years all the accompaniments of hard times were apparent on every hand. The paralysis of industry had its repercussions upon all departments of the nation's commerce, causing widespread unemployment with which neither the national nor the state and local governments were as yet prepared to cope. Private and unofficial relief agencies were unequal to the extraordinary demands made upon them, and street apple venders and beggars were everywhere in the larger communities.

Unquestionably many of the street beggars were driven to it by necessity, but the depression was the heyday of the confirmed panhandler also. They abounded on every street, day and night, in the main-traveled sections of every American city, and their solicitations were insistent and usually made on the plea of hunger or cold.

"Brother, can you spare a dime for a cup of coffee," was their theme song, and very soon it became recognized by the charitable as the shibboleth of the professional beggar. The phrase is the title and refrain of a set of verses by E. Y. Harburg, published in 1932.

"Thirty Dollars Every Thursday."

(1932)

CALIFORNIA WAS hit hard by the depression which in 1930 and 1931 was so severe as to cause a political revolution in that state. The leader of the various groups that hoped by political action to effect a reform in economic conditions was Upton Sinclair, a socialist novelist, who ran for Governor of California on a platform which advocated a system of production for use instead of one for profit. He had written a pamphlet, *End of Poverty in California,* the initials of which provided the name EPIC for the movement headed by him.

Sinclair was defeated, but the various disaffected groups that constituted his following continued, though in an imperfectly organized way, to advocate their several panaceas for social betterment. Besides the Townsendites, who advocated $200 a month old age pensions, and the Utopians, there were the Ham-and-Eggs societies, composed mainly of the unemployed. Their slogan was, "Thirty Dollars Every Thursday."

Although these groups were active and attracted many followers, they were not strong enough politically to do more than elect some local officials and state legislators.

"Tell It to Sweeney."

Leo Edward McGivena (1896-   )

In 1932, the enforced revulsion from the credit inflation of the booming 'twenties had brought a partial paralysis of consumer buying, and over-caution had succeeded reckless spending and extravagance. Inevitably the reaction was harmful to the fortunes of retail merchants. The retrenchments of consumers persisted even in the face of greatly reduced prices of needed articles not classed as luxury items.

It was the task of advertisers to overcome this sales resistance. One of the most striking examples of the efforts to this end was the full-page advertisement written by L. E. McGivena, which appeared in *The News,* New York, early in 1932. It was captioned: "Tell It to Sweeney—The Stuyvesants don't care—much." Its argument was that advertising copy, to be effective, must be directed to the great middle class, represented by the Sweeneys, rather than by the Stuyvesants.

The former were depicted as solid, fairly-prosperous, average families who had never experienced sudden wealth, had always lived within their means and found no necessity to retrench in their expenditures because of the depression. Contrasted were the ways of the Stuyvesants whose drastic retrenchments, while not really such as to lower their standards of living, gave retail advertisers scant hope of having them for their market. The plain inference to be drawn from the advertisement was that the Sweeneys, not the Stuyvesants, were the backbone of retail business.

"Tell It to Sweeney" was effective borrowing from current slang, and the copy was described by the publishers as not so much an advertisement as an idea which they developed into many similar promotional appeals.

"The forgotten man."

Franklin Delano Roosevelt

As THE panic of 1929 stretched into 1932, Franklin D. Roosevelt, then Governor of New York, became a leading candidate for the Democratic nomination for the Presidency. The widespread dislocation of industry, mounting unemployment and generally impaired prosperity of the country were every day increasing the popular dissatisfaction with President Hoover's administration and it became evident that the Democratic presidential nomination was a prize well worth striving for.

In a campaign speech delivered over the radio from Albany, New York, on April 7, 1932, just a few months before the date of the Democratic national convention, Governor Roosevelt declared that the emergency facing the nation was graver than that which confronted it in 1917. He added that it called for "plans like those of 1917 that build from the bottom up and not from the top down, that put their faith once more in the forgotten man at the bottom of the economic pyramid."

William Graham Sumner, professor of Political and Social Science, Yale University, delivered an address in 1885 with the title "The Forgotten Man." Of him he said: "The Forgotten Man works and votes—generally he prays —but his chief business in life is to pay. . . . Who and where is the Forgotten Man in this case, who will have to pay for it all?"

"The Nation's Dust Bowl."

(1933)

YEARS OF wastefulness of natural resources, unscientific farming methods and, in general, the lack of a prudent conservation policy were paid for in May 1933, by ruinous dust storms that swept over territory west of the Mississippi Valley. Stirred by high prevailing winds, tons of dust from parched and grassless acres were displaced and dumped upon thousands of acres of growing crops, destroying them and impoverishing their owners. Live stock in great numbers was lost, farm homes were engulfed, food, clothing and house furnishings were ruined, and public health impaired by the heavy clouds of dust which darkened towns, cities and the countryside and sifted down incessantly both by day and night. Not until the rains came after a protracted drought was the plague abated.

The devastated region, in which the Dakotas, Iowa, Kansas, and Nebraska were the greatest sufferers, came to be known as "The Nation's dust bowl," a graphic characterization of an area which, for the most part, had been denuded of grass by over-grazing, plowing under and the erosion caused by the clearing for timber of countless acres of wooded lands. The result of all this was an extension eastward of the "poor country" of the West with its causative aridity and high winds.

Out of the drastic experience of 1933, proceeded a national conservation program providing for reforestation and more provident methods of agriculture.

"Every Man a King."

Huey Pierce Long (1893-1935)

IN THE few years that Huey Long, successively Governor of Louisiana and United States Senator from that state, was a prominent figure in public life he acquired an enormous following, not only in his own State but throughout the nation. His followers, for the most part, were those whose poverty or lack of prosperity had made them dissatisfied with the existing order of things.

Long's appeal to this class was rendered all the stronger because of the nation-wide depression that reached an acute stage in 1932. He formulated a relief program which included the demand that the federal government guarantee an annual income of $5,000 to every family in the country, thus making "Every man a king." Furthermore, Long proposed that private fortunes be limited to fifty million dollars, legacies to five million dollars, and incomes to one million dollars a year.

* * *

"We have been relegated to the horse-and-buggy definition of interstate commerce."

Franklin Delano Roosevelt

THE INVALIDATION by the Supreme Court of the United States of the National Recovery Administration, a major project of the New Deal, was a great disappointment for President Roosevelt. On May 27, 1935, the Supreme Court in an opinion in which all its members concurred declared that under the Constitution the Federal government may regulate only interstate commerce, whereas the industries and business activities regulated by N.R.A. were intrastate in their nature.

Two days after the decision was handed down President Roosevelt at a press conference in the White House made the comment on it in which he used the "horse-and-buggy" phrase.

"Share Our Wealth."

Huey Pierce Long

AN ESSENTIAL part of Senator Long's program to revolutionize the economic system of the nation was his proposal for the redistribution of its wealth. The methods by
which he proposed to accomplish this end were vague, being no more clearly stated than that the revenue to finance
his scheme would be raised by reducing "swollen fortunes
from the top." The scheme itself provided that every family in the land should receive a homestead allowance, debt-
free and of not less than one-third the average family
wealth of the country. This meant, he explained, that every
family would possess the reasonable comforts of life to a
value of from $5,000 to $6,000 a year.

To promote his idea Long conducted a vigorous campaign, particularly in the rural sections of the South.
"Share Our Wealth" clubs were formed in many parts of
the country, and in March 1934, Long claimed that: "Two
hundred and fifty-four thousand earnest men and women
are now dedicated to an unrelenting fight to divide up the
wealth of this Land of Plenty so that children will not
starve and their parents beg for crusts."

While Long's estimate of the numerical strength of his
following may have been exaggerated, the movement
started by him undoubetdly made great progress and
"Share Our Wealth" clubs were being incorporated up to
the time of his assassination in September 1935.

"Soak the Rich."

(1935)

PRESIDENT FRANKLIN D. ROOSEVELT in June, 1935, sent a
special message to the Congress recommending revision
of federal taxes. A tax bill incorporating his recommendations was passed by the Congress on August 30, following.
The measure increased estate taxes, but lowered the rates
on small corporations. It increased to 15 percent the tax
on all corporation incomes in excess of $50,000, adding a
tax of six percent on profits in excess of ten percent, with
a graduated increase to twelve percent on profits above
fifteen percent. Taxes on corporation incomes exceeding
one million dollars were graduated steeply, reaching a
rate of seventy-five percent on incomes greater than five
million dollars. Heavy tax rates were imposed on holding
companies operated for the management of private fortunes.

The measure, which was in line with the New Deal's
program for a more equitable distribution of the tax burden, was denounced by many critics of the administration
as a device to "soak the rich" and to obtain revenge upon
men of wealth who opposed the Roosevelt policies.

"We planned it that way."

Franklin Delano Roosevelt

ONE OF the phrases most often quoted by critics of the first administration of Franklin D. Roosevelt occurred in the President's address in Charleston, South Carolina, on October 23, 1935. He had toured several cities in the state and in Charleston he was received with special enthusiasm. In his address there on the campus of The Citadel, the State military college, he stated that it was generally admitted that the country was "coming back," and added:

"Yes, we are on the way back—not by mere chance, not by a turn of the cycle. We are coming back more surely than ever before because we planned it that way; and don't let anybody tell you differently."

News reports of the President's visit stated that he seemed "unembarrassed" by the fact that figures recently made public showed that only 1,300,000 of a promised 3,500,000 were at jobs. He said that he had never set a dead-line for fulfillment of the promise, and if ninety percent were employed by the end of November he would consider it satisfactory.

In the closing days of the 1936 campaign President Roosevelt's addresses in the East again emphasized the improvement in business under the New Deal. Speaking at Camden, New Jersey, he said that "human security" was a principal objective of his administration. Of the improvement in business and the greater number of jobs at better pay, he said: "None of this came by chance. It came because . . . your Administration thought things through—thought of things as a whole—planned a balanced national economy."

"Dewey's Singing School."

(1936)

RATIFICATION OF the repeal by Congress of the Eighteenth Amendment to the Constitution prohibiting the manufacture, sale, or transportation of intoxicating liquors became a fact on December 5, 1933, and spelled the passing of the bootlegging era. Very soon it was succeeded by a period of racketeering, in which criminal elements were organized for the white slave and dope traffic, the "muscling in" on labor unions and small businesses. This racketeering brought about many gang feuds, kidnapings, and murders.

Gang lawlessness had become so flagrant in New York City by 1935 Governor Herbert H. Lehman, appointed as special prosecutor for the suppression of racketeering, Thomas E. Dewey, a young attorney who had gained prominence as special assistant in the prosecution of federal criminal cases.

Dewey's fearless and vigorous attack on racketeering and racketeers struck terror into their ranks. Especially were the leaders apprehensive, for the young prosecutor singled them out as the first ones to be indicted and put on trial. Furthermore, to clinch the cases against them, he worked on the lesser and weaker members of the gang to induce them to furnish evidence against their leaders. This was done by holding the smaller fry incommunicado in an uptown hideaway. There in time they were persuaded to "come clean," or "sing," as the act of turning state's evidence was called in crooks' slang. The hideaway was known as "Dewey's Singing School," which had a singular appropriateness because the special prosecutor was noted for his fine singing voice.

"Dewey's Singing School" aided materially in the conviction of numerous gangsters and in the virtual suppression of organized racketeering. Incidentally, it led to

Dewey's election as Governor of New York in 1942, and his nomination as the Republican candidate for President in 1944.

*   *   *

"These economic royalists."

Franklin Delano Roosevelt

SOME PARTS of President Franklin D. Roosevelt's New Deal program were vigorously opposed by elements in American business. The collective bargaining clause in the short-lived National Recovery Administration, in particular, had never found general favor among large employers of labor. In his speech accepting the Democratic nomination for re-election in 1936, President Roosevelt attacked the attitude towards his administration of ultraconservative or illiberal elements in American business and industry, saying:

"The royalists of the economic order have concede that political freedom was the business of the Government, but they have maintained that economic slavery was nobody's business. . . . These economic royalists complain that we seek to overthrow the institutions of America."

"We will spend and spend, tax and tax, elect and elect."
(1936)

A NEW DEAL measure which was subjected to great criticism was the Works Project Administration. This measure, which was put into operation early in President Franklin D. Roosevelt's first administration, was designed to relieve the unemployment by providing "made work" of various kinds, for which the Government paid, and billions of dollars were expended on the program. It was part of the administration's general plan to restore prosperity.

The whole theory of the measure was condemned by many persons on various grounds. Those economists who denied that a revival of industrial effort and prosperity generally could be effected by "pump priming" and lavish spending by the Government, pronounced WPA a false and harmful system. Politicians of the party out of power saw in it a powerful machine built for the purpose of influencing votes.

Harry Hopkins, a social welfare worker, was National Administrator of WPA and thus had the direction of vast expenditures. He was a close personal friend and adviser of the President and was quoted as having said of the administration's policy: "We will spend and spend, tax and tax, elect and elect." Mr. Hopkins repeatedly denied that he had ever used the phrase, but critics of the administration asserted that, regardless of its authorship, it represented the philosophy of the New Deal. They pointed out that President Roosevelt was re-elected in 1936 by a plurality of nearly eleven million of the popular votes and the electoral votes of forty-six states, as compared to more than seven million plurality and the electoral votes of forty-two states in 1932.

"America's Sixty Families."
Robert Houghwout Jackson (1892-   )

LATE IN 1937 what was termed a "recession" halted the business and industrial recovery that had set in during President Franklin D. Roosevelt's first term. This was naturally disturbing, even embarrassing, to the administration, which had attributed the recovery to the operation of the New Deal program it had so carefully planned. The blame for the "recession" was laid by administration spokesmen to a "strike" against the Government by American capital, the control of which, they asserted, was in a comparatively few hands.

Prominent among the administration's apologists, and probably the most vigorous in expression, was Robert H. Jackson, Assistant Attorney General, head of the Anti-Trust Division of the Department of Justice, later appointed Associate Justice of the United States Supreme Court. On two occasions within a week Jackson accused American big business, as represented by an "aristocracy" of wealth, of having been responsible for the business slump. His first attack was leveled against monopolists and oligarchic wealth in a radio address, "Business Confidence and Government Policy," delivered December 26, 1937.

In this address he declared: "About one-half of the wealth of the country is in corporate form, and over half of the corporate wealth of the country is controlled by two hundred corporations, which in turn are controlled by what a commentator has called 'America's sixty families.' "

These charges were repeated by him in his address before the American Political Science Association in Philadelphia on December 29. While Jackson did not claim to have originated the phrase and explained that he used it as a symbol, its authorship generally was attributed to him.

". . . one-third of a Nation."

Franklin Delano Roosevelt

PRESIDENT FRANKLIN D. ROOSEVELT'S re-election in 1936 by an overwhelming vote was regarded as a national endorsement of his New Deal administration with its program of economic and social reform. The President's inaugural speech on January 20, 1937, made it plain that it was the purpose of his second administration to continue and amplify his policies and to correct economic inequalities still existing. A striking phrase in his address was the statement:

"I see one-third of a Nation ill-housed, ill-clad, ill-nourished."

The President's "one-third" division, only less sweeping than Jacob Riis' "other half," was seized upon by some elements as an accurate description of prevailing conditions, but by others it was questioned as more or less arbitrary and an exaggeration not supported by the facts.

"An ever normal granary."

Henry Agard Wallace (1888-   )

IN THE framing of the second Agricultural Adjustment Act, which was passed on February 16, 1938, Henry A. Wallace, Secretary of Agriculture, had a prominent part. He was, as he said, desirous of establishing "an ever normal granary" for the country, and he is largely credited with the scheme devised in the act to provide for it. The act fixed a "parity price" on crops which represented the average purchasing power of a unit of the crop during the period 1900-1914. Loans by the Government on surplus crops would be made on an amount slightly below the parity price, and repayment of the loans and sale of the surplus would be made by farmers only at such times as the market price was at parity or higher.

This, it was argued, would result in a constant balancing of supply, as the crops stored without loss of income to the farmers when there was a surplus would be available in years when a shortage existed.

"There must be a more abundant life for the masses of the people."

Franklin Delano Roosevelt

IN MANY of his public addresses, President Roosevelt showed his deep concern for the material well-being of the great mass of people. His envisionment of economic welfare was not limited to the workers of this country, but included the peoples of the world. In his address before the Conference of the International Labor Organization, delivered in the East Room of the White House on November 6, 1941, he linked the existence of world-wide peace with the attainment of the better world it is our aim to build.

"If that world is to be one in which peace is to prevail," he said, "there must be a more abundant life for the masses of the people of all countries."

On two earlier occasions the President used the phrase. The first was in his address before the Federal Council of the Churches of Christ on December 6, 1933, in which he said:

"If I were asked to state the great objective which church and state are both demanding for the sake of every man and woman and child in this country, I would say that that great objective is 'a more abundant life'."

Again the phrase occurred in the course of an informal talk at the Alabama Polytechnic Institute, Auburn, Alabama, on March 30, 1939. Alluding to the desirability of making the southern States self-supporting, he spoke of the efforts made during the six years of his administration to give these states "a balanced economy that will spell a higher wage scale, a greater purchasing power and a more abundant life than they have had in all their history."

"From under the counter."

NOT UNTIL a rationing system had been inaugurated by the government and was well under way did the American people obtain a real appreciation of the incidental inconveniences and minor hardships to civilians entailed by war. They had heard and read, of course, of the shortages of commodities, even of the necessities of life, experienced by peoples overseas and of the means adopted by their governments to spread available supplies on a fair basis over great populations. But in a land of such vast resources, great wealth, and of such never-failing plenty as had always existed here, it was inconceivable that there should be a dearth of all those things to which civilians had been accustomed.

When, therefore, rationing on a point system was established soon after we were at war with Japan, with the attendant "ceiling prices," "black markets," and "chiseling" by both buyer and seller, full compliance with regulations became a test of patriotism and public-spiritedness. Although the showing of favoritism to customers by retailers, even when the required number of points were exchanged, was a violation of the spirit if not the letter of the regulations, it was more or less common practice. When acute shortages of commodities developed many retailers conserved their supplies and sold them only to established or heavy buyers. Because this was done with a certain measure of surreptitiousness and because the scarce articles were not displayed in plain view of all, these sales to preferred customers came to be called "from under the counter" transactions.

"Milk For the Hottentots!"

(1942)

VICE-PRESIDENT HENRY A. WALLACE wrote and spoke much on topics relating to economic conditions here and abroad, with emphasis on the right of peoples everywhere to adequate food. While his sincerity and the genuineness of his altruism were unquestioned by his critics, who were many, his views were regarded by them as those of a visionary and a "starry-eyed" dreamer.

In an address delivered before the Free World Association in New York City on May 8, 1942, he said: "Modern science . . . has made it technologically possible to see that all of the people of the world get enough to eat. Half in fun and half seriously, I said the other day to Madame Litvinov [wife of the Russian Ambassador to the United States]: 'The object of this war is to make sure that everybody in the world has the privilege of drinking a quart of milk a day.' The peace must mean a better standard of living for the common man, not merely in the United States and England, but also in India, Russia, China, and Latin America—not merely in the United Nations, but also in Germany and Italy and Japan."

The impression that he had specified the Hottentots was probably drawn from a reference in his book, *The Century of the Common Man,* published in 1943, in which he said: "In our foreign investments and activities, we have an opportunity to avoid the mistakes of the 20's. At that time the United States loaned billions of dollars abroad . . . In effect, we gave away to foreign countries (perhaps even to Hottentots!) billions of dollars of our food and manufactured goods."

Before the Senate Commerce Committee in Washington on January 25, 1945, Wallace denied that he had ever advocated a daily quart of "milk for the Hottentots," that being one of the "fantasies" attributed to him, but really spoken by the president of the National Association of

Manufacturers. He explained that by his half jesting remark to Madame Litvinov he meant that the war's inception was in economic causes.

*   *   *

"Sixty Million Jobs."

Henry Agard Wallace

HENRY A. WALLACE's championship of the "common man" did not cease with the expiration of his term as Vice President in 1945. Although not solely responsible for the administration's post-war employment program, he was, next to the President, its foremost advocate. When his nomination for the cabinet position of Secretary of Commerce was before a Senate committee for consideration he appeared and explained the administration's plans for preventing widespread unemployment after the war.

In essence, the program, which represented an aspiration rather than a definitely worked-out plan, set a goal of "sixty million jobs" as necessary to the country's prosperity, with a tolerance of three million fewer as establishing a danger point. If at any time the number of those for whom free industry could provide work fell below fifty-seven million, the Government would then provide work for the unemployed.

"A workable kit of tools for the new world."

Franklin Delano Roosevelt

As a post-war measure in the interest of a stable world economy, President Franklin D. Roosevelt in a message to the Congress on March 26, 1945, recommended the renewal of the Trade Agreements Act, with authority to reduce by reciprocal agreements the existing tariff rates by fifty percent.

Failure to adopt a policy of reducing barriers to trade, he said, would result in building up in all countries vested interests in a system of restrictions, with the consequent loss to this country of an opportunity for the greater prosperity that expanding trade brings. On the other hand, he stated, adoption of this and other policies for reconstructing the world economy would make "a good beginning at creating a workable kit of tools for the new world of international cooperation to which we all look forward."

PART FOUR

POPULAR

"Tell that to the Marines."

That rivalry, good-natured for the most part, that traditionally exists between sailors of the United States Navy and the Marines apparently is a heritage from the British navy. The usual doubting retort to a "tall story," "Tell that to the Marines—the sailors won't believe it," originated in England, and on the authority of Burton Stevenson it will be found in Sir Walter Scott's *Redgauntlet* and in Lord Byron's poem, *The Island*.

While the phrase, contrary to general belief, is not American in origin, in its abbreviated form, as well as in its usual application, it has become pretty well naturalized. It is still used here to convey derisive doubt of an improbable statement or story, but without suggestion of invidious reference to the gullibility of Marines. On the contrary, the implication usually is that the reception that can be expected to be given to a yarn of the kind by hard-fisted and realistic leathernecks would be violent and emphatic.

Early in the war between the United States and Japan the phrase was the sole comment made by President Roosevelt upon extravagant and unverified claims of victory made by the Japanese.

"Be always sure you're right—then go ahead."

David Crockett (1786-1836)

FOR MOST of his adult life David Crockett was of braggart type, more or less a poseur, but in the end he died gloriously, one of the heroes massacred in the Alamo. A Tennessean-born pioneer, he was in the tradition of Daniel Boone and other border heroes of his time. He was hunter, trapper, woodsman, a teller of tall tales, a superb marksman whose skill with the rifle was legendary, and a frontiersman politician. Although unlettered, he wrote his *Autobiography*, and in it he quoted the motto he had adopted in the War of 1812: "Be always sure you're right —then go ahead."

Crockett served under Andrew Jackson in the Creek war, and later was elected to the Tennessee legislature. He was elected Representative from Tennessee in the Congress in 1828, but failed of re-election in 1831. Two years later, however, he was re-elected, and again defeated at the end of his term. He then went to Texas to engage in the fight with the Mexicans.

Crockett's unerring marksmanship is illustrated by the backwoods story of the treed raccoon which, on recognizing Crockett as the hunter, called down to him: "Don't shoot, Colonel, I'll come down. I know I'm a gone coon."

"Hitch your wagon to a star."

Ralph Waldo Emerson

In a striking phrase devoid of abstruse meaning, the shining light of New England Transcendentalism appealed for an idealistic concept of effort. Ralph Waldo Emerson's advice, "Hitch your wagon to a star," occurs in his essay on "Civilization" in *Society and Solitude,* and as a motto it vies with that favorite of high school graduating classes: *Ad astra per ardua* (To the stars through difficulties).

The gravamen of the essay's argument is that work actuated solely by materialistic considerations, or conducted in dishonest or dishonorable manner, cannot hope to enjoy the favor or help of the gods, all of whose teams will be found "going the other way." Hence, the philosopher advises, work should be done with high motives in view, for those interests honored and promoted by the divinities: love, freedom, knowledge, utility.

"Go West, young man, and grow up with the country."
Horace Greeley (1811-1872)

It was to be expected that Horace Greeley, editor of the New York *Tribune* and keen student and observer of current history, should readily perceive the great part that the West would have in the development of the nation. He had traveled extensively through the country beyond the Mississippi, had marveled at its wealth of natural resources, and was convinced that it offered almost unlimited opportunities for those who would settle there.

Through the editorial columns of the *Tribune*, as well as in letters to and conversations with friends, he expressed his belief in the West as a profitable field for young pioneering spirits. When an editorial, "Go West, young man, go West," by John B. L. Soule, editor of the Terre Haute (Indiana) *Express*, appeared in that newspaper in 1851, Greeley reprinted it in the *Tribune*. Later in correspondence with a friend he repeated the advice, "Go West, young man," and in an editorial he added the counsel, "and grow up with the country." Although the phrase originated with Soule, who was so credited by Greeley, the greater prominence and prestige of Greeley caused it to be attributed to him.

"The only good Indian is a dead Indian."

Philip Henry Sheridan (1831-1888)

AFTER HIS service in the Civil War, in which he won
fame as one of the great cavalry leaders in the Union
Army, General Philip H. Sheridan was successively military governor in the South and in command of the Department of the Missouri. The department included a
vast area of the West which was only beginning to be
settled on any considerable scale by homesteaders.

The settlers were constantly being harassed by maraud-
ing bands of the Indian tribes whose reservations were
located in the area embraced by the Department of the
Missouri. Much of Sheridan's duties consisted of suppress-
ing these raids and his operations against the Cheyennes,
Comanches, Arapahoes and Kiowas forced them to settle
in the reservations allotted to them by treaty with the
Government.

The famous remark attributed to Sheridan, as related
by Edward Sylvester Ellis, occurred on the occasion of the
general's meeting with the Comanche Chief Toch-a-way
at old Fort Cobb in the Indian Territory in January, 1869.

Toch-a-way on being presented to Sheridan remarked,
"Me good Indian," to which Sherman is said to have replied: "The only good Indians I ever saw were dead."
Another version, more generally accepted, is, "The only
good Indian is a dead Indian."

"Who Struck Billy Patterson?"

IT HAS never been determined who, if anyone, struck Billy Patterson, or why, or where, or when. In fact, it has not been settled whether Billy Patterson ever had existence other than mythological, along with the legendary and amazing Paul Bunyan.

Researchers in American folklore and folkways have endeavored unsuccessfully to discover the origin of this phrase, which has been popularly adopted as one connoting any argument about something that probably never happened, or about some one who never existed.

Burton Stevenson concludes that it is difficult to verify any of several versions of the origin of the phrase. One that he cites gives the locale as Baltimore and the occasion a street row in which one Billy Patterson was hit and went around demanding to know who had struck him. Another version related that a medical student had been frightened to death when he imagined that he had been struck a blow. At the inquest upon his death the question uppermost was "Who struck Billy Patterson?", which was supposedly the student's name. The verdict was that no one had struck him.

"Boston is a state of mind."

(1836)

NEW ENGLAND'S Transcendental School, many of whose leaders were residents of Boston, served to fix that city in the public mind as the intellectual capital of the nation. Formed in 1836, the school itself, in which Ralph Waldo Emerson, Nathaniel Hawthorne, Bronson Alcott, George William Curtis, and Margaret Fuller were shining lights, had besides several other men and women of genius, writers, philosophers, original thinkers, social reformers, and advocates of a way of life far different from the conventional pattern. By others than the followers of Transcendentalism they were regarded as somewhat erratic and visionary, an opinion which was confirmed by the experiment of Brook Farm, a community near Boston organized on Fourier's principles for the reconstruction of society.

Because Boston was for so long the country's literary center and prided itself on this fact rather than upon the possession of purely physical features, it was characterized as "a state of mind" rather than a community in space. The witticism has been attributed variously to Emerson, Mark Twain, and Daniel Appleton, a publisher, and may well have been uttered by any one or all of them in conversation, but credit for originating it has not been assigned definitely.

"Mrs. O'Leary's Cow."

(1871)

THE MOST famous cow in history had a real existence, but the assigned basis of her fame probably is a myth. The cause of the fire that destroyed the city of Chicago in 1871, has been attributed to the celebrated animal, but probably without justification.

The account current at the time of the fire, which for a long time was accepted by many as authentic, was that on the night of October 9 a Mrs. O'Leary, who with her husband lived in a shanty in a poor section of Chicago, had gone to the barn to see that all was well with their cow, and there the lighted lantern she carried was kicked over by the cow. Barn and cow were destroyed in the resultant fire which spread to the flimsy wooden structures that abounded in the city and laid it in ruins. The story was denied by Mrs. O'Leary herself, who testified under oath that she was asleep in bed when the fire started and only learned of it when awakened by a friend.

The fire raged for more than twelve hours, ravaging an area of three and a half square miles, including the business section and much of the western and northern areas of the city, destroying 17,000 buildings with a loss of about three hundred lives and $200,000,000 in property.

"There's a sucker born every minute."
                    Phineas Taylor Barnum (1810-1891)

AMERICAN CREDULITY during the nation's age of inno-
cence was the stock in trade of Phineas T. Barnum, an
American showman who became a pioneer in the field of
vivid and extravagant advertising. Barnum was only
twenty-four years old when he bought Joyce Heath, a
colored woman who asserted that she was 161 years old
and had been a nurse of George Washington.

Barnum's success in his initial venture into humbugging
led him to purchase Scudder's American Museum in New
York City in 1841. In this gathering place of human freaks,
animal monstrosities of questionable authenticity and
assorted wonders and horrors, Barnum exhibited the
"wooly-horse," the "Feejee Mermaid," and the "Egress,"
which latter the wondering crowds eventually discovered
to be nothing more than a sign to lure them to an exit so
that a new influx of visitors might be admitted. The
showman's most successful attraction was the dwarf, General Tom Thumb, an exhibit that was genuine insofar
at least as his diminutive stature was concerned.

Barnum was a shrewd student of his fellow Americans,
and he knew them to be tolerant, easy-going and good
natured, ready to laugh at their own credulity when it
was exposed. Barnum depended for his continued success
upon the fact, as he declared, that "There's a sucker born
every minute."

He was never averse to being regarded as an ex-
ponent of the art of bamboozling people, and he lec-
tured in England on "The Science of Money Making and
the Philosophy of Humbugging." His revealing *Autobiography* and, later, his book *The Humbugs of the
World* both attest his pride in being an expert in the art.

"Without pride of ancestry or hope of posterity."

Ignatius Donnelly (1831-1901)

RESORT TO biology in the animal world was responsible
for a famous epigram by a political orator characterizing
the opposition party. Ignatius Donnelly, writer of erudite
books, journalist, politician, and witty speaker formidable
in debate, in a speech before the Minnesota legislature
declared: "The Democratic party is like a mule—without
pride of ancestry or hope of posterity." The allusion, of
course, was to the hybrid nature and sterility of the mule.

Donnelly's career in politics was brilliant but varied.
At the age of twenty-eight years he was elected Lieutenant-
Governor of Minnesota and served two terms in that office.
He served three terms as Representative in the Congress,
but after his defeat for re-election in 1870, he devoted
himself to writing. Re-entering politics, he was elected to
the Minnesota Senate and headed the powerful Farmers'
Alliance which he led into the Populist Party, of which
he was one of the founders and his been called the father.
He was nominated for the Vice-Presidency by the People's
Party in 1898.

"Politics makes strange bedfellows."

Charles Dudley Warner (1829-1900)

EXCEPT AS an observer, Charles Dudley Warner was not greatly interested in politics. Yet he is the originator of a witty quip on the subject. As a laconic commentary on the ways of politicians, their compromises, and the association of diverse elements the practice of their trade entails, the shrewd truth of his remark has been recognized generally and has caused it to be frequently quoted.

Warner's observation that "Politics makes strange bedfellows," was in the nature of an aside having little or nothing to do with the context, and was used in a little essay in *My Summer in a Garden* on his experiences as an amateur gardener.

John Spencer Bassett used the phrase, unquoted, in his *Life of Andrew Jackson,* but it is obvious that he did not originate it, as the book was not published until 1916.

Warner was the author of several books and co-author with Mark Twain of *The Gilded Age.* The often quoted witticism that, although there are always many complaints about the weather, nobody ever does anything about it, which is generally credited to Mark Twain, is believed to have been Warner's.

"I'm from Missouri, You've Got to Show Me."
Willard Duncan Vandiver (1852-   )

ABOUT THE turn of the century Missouri became known pretty generally among the sisterhood of States as the "Show Me State." Prior to that time Missourians had been tagged, particularly in the West, with the label, which was employed usually in a sense more or less derisive, implying, if not obtuseness, at least a lack of ready understanding. A currency rather more than local or sectional was given to it by Willard D. Vandiver, of Columbia, Missouri, representative in the Congress from 1897 to 1905.

While disavowing any positive claim that he originated the expression, Mr. Vandiver described the occasion upon which he used it in a public speech, following which it soon became widely used, not only in the United States, but abroad as well.

In 1902, he and other members of the Naval Committee of the House conducted an inspection of the Navy Yard in Philadelphia. The congressional inspection was made the occasion of a dinner tendered the visitors by the Five O'clock Club of Philadelphia, at which various members of the committee were called upon for speeches. Mr. Vandiver's speech was wholly informal and in light mood and in the course of it he jocularly challenged a statement by a preceding speaker from Iowa, declaring: "I'm from Missouri, you've got to show me."

In subsequent comment it was regarded as the unofficial slogan of the State, indicating the quality of insistence by hard-headed Missourians upon the production of proof of assertions. By tacit consent, it came to be considered as identifying anyone using it as, in the dictionary definition, "one not easily taken in."

"Nature-Fakers."

Theodore Roosevelt

About 1900 a great many books were being published
that dealt in an imaginative way with the habits, actions
and general behavior of various members of the animal
kingdom. Some of these books evoked adverse criticism
of the authors because it was considered they invested the
fauna of the country with remarkable qualities which were
related as fact rather than as fiction.

John Burroughs and Theodore Roosevelt were among
those most irritated by these books. The naturalist attacked their authors in an article, "Real and Sham Natural
History," which was published in 1903.

Some years later the chroniclers of amazing examples
of animal intelligence continued to irk President Roosevelt. In the Spring of 1907 Edward B. Clark of the Chicago *Evening Post,* who had been privileged to accompany
Roosevelt on some of the long hikes he enjoyed, was
visiting at the White House. At Clark's suggestion, Roosevelt permitted him to incorporate in a magazine article
his ideas about the stories he objected to. Roosevelt himself added several hundred words to the article, which
was published in *Everybody's* in June 1907 with the title,
"Roosevelt on Nature-Fakirs." The President later wrote
an article on the same subject, using the more accurate
designation "Nature-Fakers," which was published in
Everybody's in September.

The article singled out for criticism Jack London and
William J. Long, a Congregational minister, author of
several nature stories,

"Get a Horse!"

(1905)

IN MAKING its way to popular favor the automobile had to overcome much initial skepticism, some prejudice and, on occasion, considerable derision. The "horseless carriage," evolved after many experiments reaching back to the late eighteenth century, was not indeed an unqualified success. The principle of auto-propulsion, it is true, had been established, for the thing actually did run of its own motive power, but in order to keep it running a great deal remained to be done toward perfecting its engine.

The first "horseless carriage" seen in the early years of this century was a weird-looking contraption that attracted wondering and sometimes amused attention whenever and wherever it appeared. Generally, it was not taken too seriously as a practicable means of locomotion. But as improvements were made upon it and its operators ventured beyond the streets of the city out upon the roads of rural districts, it became a feared and hated thing by the farmers whose horses it frightened.

Because of the frequent break-downs of cars upon country roads, the mocking cry "Get a horse," became a commonplace, for that was the only recourse left to the stranded motorist. The spectacle of a stalled motor car being drawn over roads and streets invariably moved unsympathetic wayfarers to offer advice already taken by the motorist.

Not until the era of powerful roadsters and ubiquitous "Tin Lizzies" had been well established were the skeptical convinced that the advice was no longer needed.

"Where's the fire?"

Perhaps the first several thousand automobile speeders who were stopped by traffic policemen and asked the question, "Where's the fire?" may have taken the question seriously. But with the passage of time and the growth of motor traffic, the question became stock with the men of the traffic squads, and its heavy-handed sarcasm of dire import to offending drivers. Every speeding motorist halted by a policeman and accosted with the phrase knew immediately that it was the prelude to either a ticket or a warning lecture—or both.

*   *   *

"What this country really needs is a good five-cent cigar."
Thomas Riley Marshall (1854-1925)

ONE OF the most popular American homely epigrams was born of official ennui occasioned by a dreary and long-drawn out debate. Thomas Riley Marshall, former Governor of Indiana, and Vice President of the United States during President Wilson's two terms, was noted for his dry wit, an unfailing sense of humor and a kindly and genial manner. As Vice President he was presiding officer of the Senate. During a tiresome debate in that body on the needs of the country, the Vice President interjected the remark:

"What this country really needs is a good five-cent cigar."

"Who's loony now?"

John Armstrong Chaloner (1862-   )

FAMILY FEUDS and the escapades of the rich and socially prominent, while they are usually the subject of public comment and criticism, customarily are not pilloried by their own members. An exception was that by John Armstrong Chaloner, member of a wealthy New York family and the possessor of some wealth in his own right. A graduate of Columbia University, a lawyer, of erratic temperament, he had adopted the ancient spelling of the family name, Chanler, calling himself Chaloner.

He was constantly at odds with the members of his immediate family, and their differences were climaxed when in 1896, after he was divorced from Amelie Rives, novelist, whom he married in 1888, he was adjudged insane and committed to Bloomingdale asylum in New York. He escaped from this institution after four years' incarceration and fled to Virginia, in which State and in North Carolina he was legally declared sane.

He continued his quarrel with his family and wrote much in condemnation of its members and of the lunacy laws. When in December 1911 announcement was made of the separation of his brother Robert and Lina Cavalieri, opera prima donna, Chaloner sent an exulting telegram to his brother, asking:

"Who's loony now?"

Chaloner was gratified by the notoriety given the telegram, and in at least one of his books he repeatedly refers to himself as the author of the phrase.

"Long-haired men and short-haired women."

(1920)

IN THE decade just after the close of World War I the spirit of revolt dominating many among the younger generation had manifestations of diverse and often bizarre character. Greenwich Village, an area of vaguely defined limits in lower west side New York, was a concentration point for groups and cliques of the more pronounced rebels.

Here in dingy cellar cafes and in the garrets and converted studio apartments that abounded among the venerable residences which survived from an age of bourgeois families, nightly were gathered members of the intelligentsia, the self-styled intellectuals who were pleased to live and work in what they believed to be a bohemian atmosphere. Included in this set were exponents of new and revolutionary art forms in literature, as well as non-conformist poets, artists, painters and sculptors of unconventional schools, or no schools at all; doctrinaire preachers of strange philosophies and exponents of exotic cults; radicals, less radical "pinks" and "fellow travelers"; and a variety of others whose sympathies and professional beliefs defied exact classification.

Undoubtedly there were among them some who were sincere, but it is probably quite as certain that there were others who were exhibitionists spurred to ever greater extravagances as the Village gained notoriety. The phrase "Long-haired men and short-haired women" antedated the palmy days of the Village, but an amused public adopted it to designate the bohemian men who ostentatiously displayed their indifference to personal appearance, and their women opposites by whom bobbed hair was favored long before it became the prevailing mode.

"Take it Easy."

(1933)

THIS SENTENTIOUS American version of the old proverb, "Easy does it," may be more than merely a counsel of calm. At any rate it gained its greatest currency in the troubled years following the great business depression that began late in 1929.

By some critics of the New Deal, especially of the Works Projects Administration, it was regarded as an appropriate motto for relief workers engaged on "made work" projects where speed would endanger the continuance of their jobs.

But the phrase has survived WPA, and has become a favorite admonition as a form of farewell between friends.

*   *   *

Boon Doggles."

(1935)

AS PART of the terminology of the Great Depression the word "Boondoggling" was adopted enthusiastically by the American press and public to describe relief projects in the nature of made work of dubious value.

The word was revealed during an aldermanic inquiry in 1935 into the operations of relief administration in New York City, in the course of which Robert Marshall, who described himself as a "training specialist," testified that he taught those on relief "boon doggles." This, he explained, was a long-standing pioneer designation for tricks of handicraft, such as making belts by weaving ropes, and the like.

"Say it ain't so, Joe."

(1920)

THE WORLD SERIES of 1919 developed the greatest scandal in the history of organized baseball. The contest that year was between the Cincinnati Reds, of the National League, and the Chicago White Sox, of the American League. The series was won by the Cincinnati team by five games out of the eight played.

The suspicions of followers of the national game were aroused toward the end of the series by the actions of certain of the players, and for months thereafter there were rumors that the series had been "fixed" in the interest of gamblers. The story of the scandal was not revealed until September 20, when detectives employed by Charles Comiskey, manager of the Chicago team, established that eight players on that team had been paid by gamblers to "throw" the series to the Cincinnati team. The accused men were brought up on charges before a trial body of organized baseball, found guilty and barred from baseball for life.

One of the men was Joe Jackson, a great batter and the idol of baseball fans everywhere. His disgrace gave currency to a phrase which has become a classic, "Say it ain't so, Joe," supposed to have been uttered by a tearful urchin who stopped Jackson as he left the room where he had faced the charges. Jackson, the legend relates, hung his head in shame and was silent.

Whether apocryphal or not, the story was generally accepted as fact and has been adopted as a footnote of baseball history.

BIBLIOGRAPHY

SAMUEL HOPKINS ADAMS. *The Incredible Era: the Life and Times of Warren Gamaliel Harding.* Boston. 1929.

FREDERICK L. ALLEN. *Since Yesterday.* New York. 1940.

AMERICAN LEGION MAGAZINE, January 1933. *40,000 Men and o Horses,* by John A. Elden.

JOHN BARTLETT. *Familiar Quotations,* edited by Christopher Morley and Louella D. Everett. Boston. 1941.

JOHN SPENCER BASSETT. *Life of Andrew Jackson.* Garden City, N. Y. 1911.

CHARLES A. and MARY BEARD. *A Basic History of the United States.* Philadelphia. 1944.

CLAUDE M. BOWERS. *Jefferson and Hamilton.* Boston. 1925.

VAN WYCK BROOKS. *The World of Washington Irving.* New York. 1944.

WILLIAM BROWN. *Captains of the Civil War.* New Haven. 1921.

B. A. BOTKIN, editor. *A Treasury of American Folklore.* New York. 1944.

AUGUSTUS C. BUELL. *History of Andrew Jackson,* 2 v. New York, 1904.

California, The, Workingmen's Party. San Francisco. 1878.

OLIVER CARLSON and ERNEST S. BATES. *Hearst, the Lord of San Simeon.* New York. 1936.

ARTHUR CHAPMAN. *Out Where the West Begins, and Other Western Verses.* Boston. 1917.

DONALD BARR CHIDSEY. *The Gentleman from New York.* New Haven. 1935.

MEYER COHEN. *Selected Decisions of the Supreme Court.* New York. 1937.

JOSEPHUS DANIELS. *The Wilson Era.* Chapel Hill, N. C. 1944.

HENRY KELSEY DEVEREUX. *The Spirit of '76.* Cleveland. 1926.

DICTIONARY OF AMERICAN BIOGRAPHY. Dumas Malone, editor. New York. 1935.

FINLEY PETER DUNNE. *Mr. Dooley at His Best,* edited by Elmer Ellis. New York. 1943.

ENCYCLOPEDIA AMERICANA. New York. 1941.

ENCYCLOPEDIA BRITTANICA. Fourteenth edition. London and New York. 1930.

FOREST AND STREAM, January 1928. *The Master of Woodchuck Lodge*, by Henry Fitzwilliam Woods.

HOWELL M. FORGY. *And Pass the Ammunition*. New York. 1944.

ROBERT H. FULLER. *Jubilee Jim*. New York. 1928.

JAMES SLOAN GIBBONS. *The Manuscript of "We are Coming, Father Abraham."* New York. 1942.

JOSEPH C. GREW. *Ten Years in Japan*. New York. 1944.

ROLAND HILL HARVEY. *Samuel Gompers*. Stanford University Press. 1935.

LAWRENCE HALL HEALY and LUIS KUTNER. *The Admiral*. New York. 1944.

ROBERT SELPH HENRY. *"First With the Most" Forrest*. Indianapolis. 1944.

STEWART H. HOLBROOK. *None More Courageous*. New York. 1942.

EMILY KATHARINE IDE. *The History and Significance of the American Flag*. Cambridge. 1917.

WASHINGTON IRVING. *Captain Bonneville*. New York. n.d.

MARQUIS JAMES. *Jackson, Portrait of a President*. Indianapolis. 1937.

GEORGE O'BRIEN JOHN. *Texas History, an Outline*. New York. 1935.

VIRGIL CARRINGTON JONES. *Ranger Mosby*. Chapel Hill, N. C. 1944.

MATTHEW JOSEPHSON. *The Robber Barons*. New York. 1934.

JAMES KELLER and MEYER BERGER. *Men of Maryknoll*. New York. 1943.

JAMES KERNEY. *The Political Education of Woodrow Wilson*. New York. 1926.

FRANK KINGDON. *That Man in the White House*. New York. 1944.

WILLIAM CHAUNCEY LANGDON. *Everyday Things in American Life*. New York. 1941.

ROBERT LAWSON. *Watchwords of Liberty*. Boston. 1943.

LLOYD LEWIS. *Sherman, Fighting Prophet*. New York. 1932.

LITERARY DIGEST, January 28, 1922; April 13, 1917. *The Roosevelt-Harrison Imbroglio*.

ROBERTUS LOVE. *The Rise and Fall of Jesse James*. New York. 1926.

COMPTON MACKENZIE. *Mr. Roosevelt.* New York. 1944.

EDGAR STANTON MACLAY. *Life and Adventures of "Jack" Philip.* New York. 1903.

THOMAS RILEY MARSHALL. *Recollections.* Indianapolis. 1925.

JOHN McCONAUGHEY. *Who Rules America?* New York. 1934.

ROBERT McELROY. *Grover Cleveland, the Man and the States-man.* New York. 1923.

CHARLES MICHELSON. *The Ghost Talks.* New York. 1944.

GEORGE FORT MILTON. *The Use of Presidential Powers.* Boston. 1944.

JAMES MORGAN. *Our Presidents.* New York. 1928.

DAVID S. MUZZEY. *History of the American People.* Boston. 1934.

GUSTAVE MYERS. *The History of Great American Fortunes.* Chicago. 1910.

ALLAN NEVINS. *Grover Cleveland; a Study in Courage.* New York. 1933.

NEW STANDARD ENCYCLOPEDIA. New York. 1931.

NEW YORK TIMES MAGAZINE, April 1, 1945. *Are Women Persons?* by Edith Efron.

JAMES PARTON. *Life of Aaron Burr.* Boston. 1886.

JAMES PARTON. *Life of Horace Greeley.* Boston. 1889.

REMBERT W. PATRICK. *Jefferson Davis and His Cabinet.* Baton Rouge, La. 1945.

FREDERIC L. PAXSON. *America at War, 1917-1918.* Boston. 1939.

FREDERIC L. PAXSON. *History of the American Frontier.* 1763-1893. Boston. 1924.

WESTBROOK PEGLER. *'Tain't Right.* New York. 1936.

ROEY V. PELL and THOMAS C. DONNELLY. *The 1928 Election.* New York. 1931.

FLETCHER PRATT. *The Heroic Years; Fourteen Years of the Republic, 1801-1815.* New York. 1934.

GEORGE H. PREBLE. *Our Flag.* Boston. 1880.

HENRY F. PRINGLE. *Theodore Roosevelt, a Biography.* New York. 1931.

MILO M. QUAIFE. *Lake Michigan.* Indianapolis. 1944.

BASIL RAUCH. *The History of the New Deal.* New York. 1944.

JAMES FORD RHODES. *History of the United States,* vol. 1. New York. 1902.

JAMES FORD RHODES. *The McKinley and Roosevelt Administrations.* New York. 1922.

EVERETT RICH. *William Allen White, the Man from Emporia.* New York. 1941.

JOSEPH M. ROGERS. *The True Henry Clay.* Philadelphia. 1904.

CARLOS P. ROMULO. *I Saw the Fall of the Philippines.* New York. 1942.

THEODORE ROOSEVELT. *An Autobiography.* New York. 1913.

THEODORE ROOSEVELT. *Fear God and Take Your Own Part.* New York. 1916.

THEODORE ROOSEVELT. *The Strenuous Life, Essays and Addresses.* New York. 1900.

WILLIAM A. SIMONDS. *Henry Ford.* New York. 1943.

MRS. CHETWOOD SMITH. *History's Most Famous Words.* New York. 1926.

J. HENRY SMYTHE, JR. *The Amazing Benjamin Franklin.* New York. 1929.

BURTON STEVENSON. *The Home Book of Quotations.* New York. 1937.

MELVILLE E. STONE. *Fifty Years a Journalist.* New York, 1921.

MARK SULLIVAN. *Our Times.* Vols. 2, 3 and 4. New York. 1927.

JOSEPH P. TUMULTY. *Woodrow Wilson as I Know Him.* New York. 1921.

FREDERICK JACKSON TURNER. *The United States, 1830-1850.* New York. 1935.

CARL VAN DOREN. *Benjamin Franklin.* New York. 1938.

STANLEY WALKER. *Dewey, an American of This Century.* New York. 1944.

HENRY A. WALLACE. *The Century of the Common Man.* New York. 1943.

CHARLES DUDLEY WARNER. *My Summer in a Garden.* Boston. 1888.

CHARLES WARREN. *Congress, the Constitution and the Supreme Court.* Boston. 1935.

M. R. WERNER. *Barnum.* New York. 1923.

EDWIN P. WHIPPLE. *The Great Speeches and Orations of Daniel Webster.* Boston. 1879.

WILLIAM ALLEN WHITE. *A Puritan in Babylon.* New York. 1938.

JENNINGS COOPER WISE. *Woodrow Wilson, Disciple of Revolution.* New York. 1938.

RALPH L. WOODS. *A Treasury of the Familiar.* New York. 1943.

INDEX OF PHRASES

INDEX OF NAMES